THE
FREEZER TO MICROWAVE
HEALTHY EATING
HANDBOOK

JILL McWILLIAM

OCTOPUS BOOKS
IN ASSOCIATION WITH BEJAM

Right: a selection of the healthy ingredients used for recipes in this book
Front cover: Corsican cannelloni (page 71) with Summer peaches (page 54)
Back cover: Kissel (page 55) with Nutty shortbread (page 45)

ACKNOWLEDGEMENTS

Recipes developed by: Kate Moseley and Sara Buenfeld

Photographers: Graham Kirk
Clive Streeter (pages 6-7, 47, 55, 74 and back cover)
Chris Crofton (front cover)

Stylist: Andrea Lambton

Food prepared for photography by: Allyson Birch
Dolly Meers (pages 6-7, 47, 55, 74)

Artwork and Illustration: Chris Lyon

The publishers would like to thank the following companies for their kindness in
providing materials and equipment used in the photography for this book:
Dickens & Jones, Regent Street, London W1
Covent Garden Kitchen Supplies, Covent Garden Piazza, London WC2
Tile With Style, 270 Kentish Town Road, London NW5
Boots Cookshop, Brent Cross, London NW9
Josiah Wedgewood and Sons, 34 Wigmore Street, London W1

NOTES

Standard spoon measurements are used in all recipes:
1 tablespoon = one 15 ml spoon
1 teaspoon = one 5 ml spoon
All spoon measures are level.
All eggs are size 3 (standard) unless otherwise stated. For all recipes, quantities are
given in both metric and imperial measures. Follow either set but not a mixture of both,
as they are not interchangeable.

All of the recipes conclude with a simple four-item dietary assessment, and these have
been specially checked by a fully qualified nutritionist. These assessments are intended
as a comparative guide only; every recipe in the book, regardless of its dietary
assessment, may be regarded as 'healthy'.

Published by Octopus Books Limited,
59 Grosvenor Street, London W1X 9DA
First published 1986
© Octopus Books 1986
ISBN 0 7064 2575 8

Reprinted 1987

Printed in Hong Kong

CONTENTS

WHAT IS HEALTHY EATING?

In a survey recently conducted by Bejam, 61 per cent of those housewives questioned in the UK said they were making a deliberate effort to improve their families' diet.

However, the survey also revealed that many housewives are confused by conflicting information from different sources and are concerned by medical reports of diet-related diseases. How are we supposed to decide whether or not butter is better than margarine? How much bran constitutes a daily requirement? Is skimmed milk the best choice? And so on and so forth: seemingly, all the 'experts' have different views.

Having tried various so-called 'health-giving' diets, I have come to the conclusion that it is not necessary to be fanatical about food. There is no need to go to extremes and introduce vast quantities of bran to increase fibre intake, or to replace *all* saturated fats with sunflower oil and margarines high in polyunsaturates. The key to healthy eating lies in a balanced approach.

The majority of foods eaten should be in their natural state. This means foods, where possible, should be eaten as whole foods, restricting refined foods such as white sugar and white flour. Include in your diet plenty of fruit, vegetables, nuts, seeds, grains, wholemeal bread, low-fat dairy products, white meat and fish. This approach to diet doesn't mean that you can't have a little of what you fancy once in a while, or have fun with your food. Of course you can, but the major part of the diet should consist of a variety of the natural foods already mentioned. In addition, all foods should be eaten in moderation, and that means not eating too much of one type of food.

Switching to a sensible healthy diet is easy, inexpensive, highly enjoyable and . . . you'll wonder why you didn't do it years ago.

J, McWilliam

THE PERFECT PAIR

Our hectic lifestyle demands that food should be easily available, and that it can be prepared and cooked quickly. In response to these demands, the freezer and microwave cooker make a perfect pair.

A healthy diet and the freezer

Any diet should be varied and interesting and a freezer can provide you with a wealth of choice, whether this choice be purchased frozen or home-made and then frozen. With the advent of the freezer, the limitations of seasonal availability have become a thing of the past.

★ The most perfect way of preserving food is by freezing. This is not to suggest that frozen is better than fresh: the two simply complement each other superbly and add balance and ease to menu planning.

★ Busy, health-conscious people require the convenience of being able to cook as and when time is available. Additionally, the freezer offers the facility to store prepared items, like vegetable meals, reduced fat/sugar dishes, wholemeal bread and pastries, for use when time is short.

★ Home-grown vegetables can be frozen and used throughout the year.

A healthy diet and the microwave cooker

★ Most food, both fresh and frozen, benefits from being cooked in its own juice or in very little added liquid. Microwave cooking ensures that food retains its natural flavour and moisture.

★ Fish and poultry give particularly good results when cooked in the microwave cooker, remaining moist and tender.

★ Vegetables have always been an essential part of a balanced diet. The microwave cooker cooks them superbly with hardly any additional water or fat – hence saving valuable vitamins and minerals that may otherwise be lost during traditional cooking, and reducing fat levels. Microwave cooking brings out the full flavour of vegetables, so less salt and sauces are required.

★ The speed and efficiency of microwave cooking reduces the temptation to resort to crisps or chocolate for a snack: most healthy alternatives can be quickly prepared.

★ A 'fry up' need never take the place of a balanced meal, as defrosting and re-heating are quick and simple.

★ As the microwave cooker is perfectly safe for everyone to use, including children and the elderly, no-one need skimp or miss out on balanced meals. The simple operation of the microwave cooker has particular benefits for the disabled who may otherwise find cooking difficult in practical terms.

THE DIET OF THE 1980'S

Throughout the twentieth century there has been an awareness of the importance of diet, but the changing economic climate and subsequent improvement in lifestyle mean that what we eat has radically changed.

Having successfully overcome earlier problems of malnutrition, rickets and scurvy by improving the diet, we have now so refined what we eat that we have diet-related conditions such as obesity and possibly heart disease.

It became easy (and fashionable) to indulge in a diet rich in proteins and fats and low in dietary fibre, and this is when problems began. The 1980's diet doesn't necessarily mean a balanced diet.

The diet controversy has focused on a discussion paper prepared by the National Advisory Committee on Nutrition Education – the NACNE report. Diet 2000, a layman's interpretation of the NACNE report, recommends the following dietary changes:

1. Number of calories taken in should be appropriate for maintaining optimal body weight for height and sex, with adequate exercise.
   Being overweight is associated with all sorts of health problems, apart from any desire to look slim. Keep an eye on your weight and don't let it creep up.

2. Fat intake should be, on average, 30 per cent of total calories. The average person should aim to cut his or her total fat intake by nearly a quarter.
   Avoid fried foods, fatty sauces and dressings; spread butter or margarine sparingly.
   Saturated fat intake should be on average 10 per cent of total calories . . . this means cutting saturated fat by nearly half.
   Choose low-fat dairy produce and lean meat (remove visible fat). Eat more

chicken, fish and turkey – all low in saturated fats.

3. Average sucrose intake should be reduced to 20 kg per head per year (the average person should halve his or her consumption).
Cut down on sugar. Avoid sweets and chocolate. By cutting down gradually you can lose your sweet tooth without even feeling deprived.

4. Average salt intake should fall by 3 g per head per day – representing a 25 per cent cut.
Use salt sparingly. A few grains go a long way. The taste for salt is an acquired one, and it is easy to lose.

5. Fibre intake should increase on average to 30 g per head per day.
Eat lots of fibre-rich foods – unpeeled vegetables (particularly peas, beans and sweetcorn), fruit, wholemeal bread, potatoes, pulses and high fibre breakfast cereals.

Other recommendations are:

Alcohol – *average intake should be no more than 4 per cent of total calories (say one pint of beer or two glasses of wine per day).*

Protein – *on average, we are probably eating more than we need.*

Following all these guidelines will help provide a diet which is high in vitamins and minerals, and low in fat and cholesterol.

We have the information and the food at our disposal to improve our eating habits quickly and efficiently. As many people have already realised, this need not be expensive, nor time consuming nor gastronomically dull. Happily, we are beginning to get the healthy eating message.

FOOD LABELLING

New regulations on food labelling came into force in January 1983 as part of the EEC's consumer protection programme. The UK has had food labelling laws for many years but never any as comprehensive as they are today.

For those concerned about diet, reading food labels on pre-packed foods has become a necessary part of shopping. A little background may help to identify the important points and avoid unnecessary concern when, for example, 'E' numbers are encountered.

Ingredients panel

The ingredients panel, now compulsory on all pre-packed foods, gives a detailed breakdown of the exact contents of the food. This is recorded in descending order of weight. Added water must also be included if it comprises more than 5 per cent of the weight of the product. All food additives will be included, but remember that only tried and tested colourings, flavourings and preservatives are allowed. Many of these substances have been allocated 'E' numbers.

For example:

E440(a) is pectin, a natural ingredient from the cell walls of plants, used for centuries as a gelling agent in preserves.

E100 is turmeric, a natural root extract used for colouring foods such as rice, margarine or processed cheese. Many cooks stock turmeric for enhancing the colour and flavour of home-made dishes.

There has been much controversy surrounding certain E numbers, particularly those thought to cause hyperactivity in children. Many of these have been

eliminated voluntarily by food manufacturers and replaced by safe alternatives. One could question the need for colourings and flavouring and perhaps in the not-too-distant future we shall see many of them disappear. In general, though, food additives cause few problems and many flavourings and colourings simply serve an aesthetic function.

Preservatives are more important. They prevent many foods deteriorating between manufacture and consumption. For example, sausages have had permitted preservatives for many years, so it comes as no surprise to find them in other meat products. The only alternative would be to buy these foods for immediate consumption from a dealer of impeccable reputation – or keep your own animals.

Nutritional labelling

There is no legislation relating to nutritional labelling on packaging, except that if a food manufacturer chooses to include it on the label it must conform to certain guidelines. The increased public interest in diet has, in fact, prompted many manufacturers to include nutritional information voluntarily on packaging. Take for example the pack in the

FOOD FACTS

Serve one steak with vegetables for a delicious meal under 250 calories. Each steak provides at least one fifth of the protein recommended daily for most people.

A cooked Steak contains:

	Oven Cooked or Grilled	Shallow Fried	Deep Fried
Protein	13g	13g	13g
Fat	9g	12g	14g
Carbohydrate	12g	12g	12g
Calories	180	205	225
Calories per ounce	63	61	70

illustration above. This shows the type of useful nutritional data supplied by one manufacturer.

Other helpful information available on packaging includes:
– cooking instructions
– recipe ideas
– storage information
– display-by and sell-by dates on fresh products.

HEALTHY FREEZER HINTS

Keeping a well-stocked freezer can help you create healthier meals.

* Vegetables contain many of the vitamins, minerals and fibre needed for a healthy diet. Frozen vegetables give you varied, year-round availability, high quality and stable prices.
* Take advantage of the ready-prepared vegetable mixes. Use them in stews and casseroles or as delicious vegetable side dishes on their own.
* Peas are a family favourite and are high in fibre. Try mixing them with sweetcorn for variety in flavour and colourful presentation.
* Vegetables can make an endless variety of interesting salads. They should be lightly cooked then cooled. Try peas, sweetcorn, Veg 'n' Rice Mix and broad beans.
* A 'freezer stockpot' is invaluable, using vegetable cooking water which contains lots of nutrients. Freeze it in ice cube trays or bags and use in soup or as a casserole base.
* Pulses such as haricot beans, kidney beans, lentils etc. are an excellent source of dietary fibre. They need lengthy soaking and cooking so prepare them in quantity, freeze and re-heat as needed. Use in soups and stews or as a nourishing and filling vegetable.
* Fish is generally frozen within hours of being caught. Ring the changes and try using fish instead of meat in favourite dishes, such as cod and mushroom pie instead of steak and kidney, or smoked haddock in lasagne.
* Keep a packet of frozen prawns in the freezer. Thaw in the microwave cooker then make up prawn cocktail as a starter for a special treat. Serve with a healthy yogurt and tomato dressing instead of rich cocktail sauce.
* Use different types and cuts of meat to add variety to your diet. For example, rabbit is a white meat, low in fat and very economical. Rabbit portions and diced rabbit can be braised, fricasseed or made into a tasty pie.
* Lambs' kidneys are high in protein, minerals and vitamins, and one kidney will supply a third of an adult's daily iron requirement. They are economical to buy and make a tasty meal.
* To add flavour to meat, fish and poultry, prepare a tasty marinade using fruit juices, wine, herbs and spices, and freeze in plastic cups until needed.
* Always keep several loaves of bread in the freezer and gradually make the switch from white to wholemeal. For everyday packed lunches, plan a sandwich-making session and prepare an assortment of low-fat fillings.
* Keep a stock of fruit purées in the freezer made from fruits such as blackcurrants or raspberries. Try not to sieve soft fruits as the pips are high in fibre.
* Freeze leftover fruit, such as pineapple or melon and use to vary fish and meat dishes, or fruit desserts.
* Frozen raspberries retain their flavour and colour when thawed. Use whole to decorate desserts or purée to make a sauce, or turn into a tasty mousse or soufflé.
* Make a delicious, healthy milkshake drink by thawing and blending frozen strawberries, black cherries, or raspberries with skimmed milk.
* Ice cream is a nutritious family favourite, and is a good source of calcium. Three scoops of vanilla ice cream contain only about 130 calories!
* Freeze as many 'leftovers' as you can to avoid the temptation to nibble. Unlike the refrigerator or cupboard, the freezer deters you from casual indulgence in snacks!
* Home-made cakes freeze beautifully. If you only want one slice, cut the cake into portions before freezing. When cut, place waxed paper between the slices and freeze. Remove portions as required.
* Prepare individual portions of baby food for the freezer. It's economical, convenient and helps to provide healthy, balanced meals for the youngest members of the family.

HEALTHY WAYS WITH THE MICROWAVE COOKER

The microwave cooker not only helps you get the best from your freezer, it is also a speedy and reliable means of cooking and helps you create a variety of nutritious dishes.

* Wholesome soups and sauces are best made from home-made stock. Vegetable, fish and chicken stocks are used in many healthy recipes. They can be made quickly

and easily in the microwave, then stored in the freezer.

To make vegetable stock: place 450 g/1 lb frozen Stewpack, or an equivalent weight of fresh vegetables, including carrots, swedes, turnips, onions and celery, trimmed and diced, in a 3 litre/6 pint bowl. Add a few bay leaves and peppercorns, 1 tablespoon chopped fresh parsley and 1 tablespoon yeast extract, and cover with water. Bring to the boil on HIGH, then cook on LOW for 20 minutes. Strain and cool.

To make fish stock: place 1 kg/2 lb of fish bones, heads and trimmings in a 3 litre/6 pint bowl and cover with water. Add sprigs of fresh herbs, 1 sliced onion, 1 carrot and 1 roughly chopped stick celery, and season to taste. Bring to the boil on HIGH then cook, uncovered on LOW for 10 minutes. Strain and cool.

To make chicken stock: place a chicken carcass and giblets (excluding liver) in a 3 litre/6 pint bowl. Add a bay leaf and bouquet garni, and season with pepper. Bring to the boil on HIGH then cook uncovered on MEDIUM for 30-40 minutes. Strain and cool, then skim off any fat which has risen to the surface.

★ The delicate flavour and tender, moist texture of fish are retained when cooked in the microwave cooker. To get the best results note the following points:

Fish cooks in its own juice and requires no additional liquid.

Whole fish up to 1 kg/2 lb must be slashed 2 or 3 times across the skin on each side to allow even cooking.

Large whole fish which will not fit into a dish can be 'curled', tying the head to the tail loosely with a piece of string. This makes it possible to cook a whole salmon.

★ The microwave cooker reheats fish superbly, but take care not to overheat it or it may begin to overcook. STANDING time is important to ensure even reheating.

★ Thaw meat on DEFROST in the microwave cooker to avoid losing moisture from the meat.

★ Use only the best cuts of meat in the microwave cooker. When casseroling or stewing meat, marinate the meat first. This will enhance the flavour and help tenderize the meat.

★ Trim the fat from chops and steaks before microwave cooking. Remove the fat frequently during cooking. This is particularly important when cooking joints and larger cuts such as steaks and chops, otherwise microwave power will be wasted, cooking the meat juices and fat instead of the meat.

★ For fatty minced beef, place the meat in a plastic colander over a bowl and cook on HIGH for 3 minutes. Discard the fat and then use the mince as required.

★ To make good gravy, skim the fat from the roasting dish. Collect the cooking juices in a jug and add a couple of ice cubes. As the fat rises it clings to the ice cubes making it easy to remove. Add stock and cook on HIGH until boiling. Thicken if required. This method of skimming fat can also be applied to stews and casseroles.

★ Poultry and game benefit from the moisture-retaining qualities of microwave cooking which leave the flesh tender and succulent. Birds such as duck and goose (maximum size 5.5 kg/12 lb) should be well cooked and the fat drained at frequent intervals. Remove the skin before serving.

★ The high water content of vegetables, whether fresh or frozen, means that very little water is used for cooking, which in turn means that less nutrients are lost. Vegetables such as spinach, cabbage, tomatoes and courgettes require no added liquid. Podded vegetables such as peas or broad beans, as well as sweetcorn, require a few tablespoons of water in cooking.

★ Microwave cooking retains the true flavours of vegetables so little or no salt is needed. If salt is necessary add it to the vegetables after cooking.

★ No extra water is required when stewing fresh or frozen fruit. The flavour of the fruit is therefore completely natural and undiluted. When cooking dried fruits, which are an excellent substitute when fresh fruit is unavailable, there is no need to pre-soak the fruit. Allow sufficient water during cooking to allow for absorption.

★ Plated meals can be cooked or reheated in minutes, with no loss of flavour or good-ness: no more dried remnants for latecomers.

★ For single people or dieters the microwave is ideal for cooking or reheating small portions of food, quickly and economically.

HEALTHY MEAT AND POULTRY

The recipes that follow show you meat cookery at its healthiest, using lean cuts of meat and cooking them with less fat in the microwave cooker. Poultry also plays a significant role in a healthy diet. It is low in fat and stays particularly succulent when cooked in the microwave cooker.

Chicken pâté ring

Serves 6-8
225 g/8 oz frozen chicken livers, defrosted
100 g/4 oz frozen onion slices, or 1 small
    fresh onion, peeled and sliced
2 cloves garlic, roughly chopped
2 teaspoons chopped fresh thyme, or
    1 teaspoon dried thyme
1 egg
1 tablespoon brandy
freshly ground black pepper
25 g/1 oz fresh wholemeal breadcrumbs
225 g/8 oz frozen boneless diced chicken
    breast, defrosted and minced
To garnish
50 g/2 oz fresh watercress
4 button mushrooms, thinly sliced
lemon wedges
tomato wedges

1 Place the chicken livers, onion slices, garlic and thyme in a food processor or blender and process until finely chopped.

2 Add the egg, brandy, pepper and breadcrumbs. Process for a few more seconds then add the chicken.

3 Lightly grease an 18 cm/7 inch ring mould with a little vegetable oil. Alternatively use a soufflé dish with a straight sided glass, base down, in the centre.

4 Carefully spoon in the pâté mixture. Cover with cling film, pierce, and cook on MEDIUM for 8 minutes. STAND for 5 minutes then cook on MEDIUM for 2 minutes.

5 Leave covered until cold. If necessary, remove the glass from the centre of the dish. Turn the pâté out of the mould or dish.

6 To serve, fill the centre of the ring with fresh watercress and garnish with the sliced button mushrooms, and lemon and tomato wedges.

To freeze: the pâté can be turned out, wrapped in a double layer of cling film and frozen. Thaw in the refrigerator for about 6 hours.

Note: this pâté is best made the day before serving.

Fibre	● ●	Sugar	●
Fat	● ●	Salt	●

Mulligatawny soup

Serves 4
1 tablespoon curry powder
2 tablespoons tomato purée
50 g/2 oz long grain brown rice
600 ml/1 pint chicken stock, heated to
    boiling
175 g/6 oz frozen onion slices, or 2 small
    fresh onions, peeled and sliced
2 cloves garlic, crushed
100 g/4 oz frozen apple slices
freshly ground black pepper
50 g/2 oz red pepper, cored, seeded and cut
    into strips
50 g/2 oz cooked chicken, skinned and cut
    into strips

Chicken pâté ring

1 Blend the curry powder with the tomato purée in a very large bowl. Cook on HIGH for 1 minute.

2 Add the rice, stock, onion, garlic and apple. Stir well, then season with plenty of black pepper.

3 Cover with cling film and pierce. Cook on HIGH for 15 minutes stirring halfway through the cooking time.

4 Stir in the red pepper and chicken then cook on HIGH for a further 5 minutes.

To freeze: cool, then pack into a rigid container and label. Use within 3 months. To thaw and reheat from frozen, place the block in a large bowl. Cover with cling film, pierce, and reheat on HIGH for 15-20 minutes breaking up the block of soup as it thaws.

Note: for a vegetarian soup, omit the chicken and use a vegetable stock cube or make home-made vegetable stock. Follow the recipe on page 9.

| Fibre | ● | Sugar | ● |
| Fat | ● | Salt | ● ● |

Tandoori-style chicken

Serves 4
8 large frozen chicken drumsticks, about
75 g/3 oz each, defrosted
For the marinade
4 tablespoons natural yogurt
3 tablespoons light red tandoori
spice mixture
1 tablespoon lemon juice
1 tablespoon white wine vinegar

1 Skin the chicken and prick the flesh all over with a fork. Place the chicken in a bowl. Combine the marinade ingredients, then spoon over the chicken drumsticks until they are evenly coated. Leave to stand in the marinade for at least 1 hour or preferably overnight so that the flavours penetrate the meat.

2 Arrange the chicken drumsticks, radiating out from the centre of a large round plate, making sure the thickest parts are on the outside of the plate.

3 Cook, uncovered on HIGH for 8 minutes. Leave to STAND for 5 minutes then pierce with a sharp knife or skewer. The juices should be clear. Return any pieces where the juices are not running clear to the microwave cooker, and cook for a further minute.

4 Serve the tandoori-style chicken with a fresh green salad and lemon wedges and poppadoms, as part of an Indian-style meal.

To freeze: cool, pack in a rigid container and label. Use within 1 month. To serve, thaw on DEFROST for 8 minutes. Reheat on HIGH for 3-5 minutes until hot.

Note: poppadoms are large crisp Indian breads and can be cooked healthily and successfully in the microwave cooker. Place four at a time in a single layer on the floor of the microwave cooker. Cook uncovered, on HIGH, for 1½-2 minutes.

Fibre		**Sugar**	●
Fat	●	**Salt**	●

Lemon chicken in mushroom sauce

Serves 4
8 frozen part-boned chicken thighs,
defrosted and skinned
25 g/1 oz butter
1 tablespoon chopped fresh parsley
1 tablespoon chopped fresh tarragon or 2
teaspoons dried tarragon
100 g/4 oz frozen sliced mushrooms
2 teaspoons cornflour blended with 1
tablespoon lemon juice
2 tablespoons natural yogurt
To garnish
grated rind of ½ lemon
1 tablespoon chopped fresh parsley

1 Arrange the chicken thighs in a shallow dish. Put the butter and herbs into a small bowl. Cook on HIGH for ½-1 minute then brush over chicken pieces.

2 Cover the chicken with cling film, pierce, and cook on HIGH for 5 minutes. Turn the joints over, cover again and cook on HIGH for a further 3-4 minutes or until the chicken juices run clear.

3 Transfer the chicken to a hot serving plate. Keep warm. Add the mushrooms and blended cornflour to the chicken juices, cover again and cook on HIGH for 1 minute. Carefully stir in the yogurt.

4 Return the chicken to the microwave cooker and cook on HIGH for 1-2 minutes to heat through if necessary. Pour the sauce over the chicken and sprinkle with lemon rind and parsley.

5 Serve on a bed of Brown rice (page 32) with Julienne of vegetables (page 36).

To freeze: not suitable for freezing.

Variations
Turkey breast slices, or chicken breast portions, frozen and defrosted, could be used in this recipe instead of chicken.

Fibre	●	**Sugar**	●
Fat	● ●	**Salt**	●

Pork rolls with apple and prune stuffing

Serves 4
2 × 225 g/8 oz lean pork steaks
100 g/4 oz frozen onion slices, or 1 small
   fresh onion, peeled and finely sliced
4 prunes, stoned and cut into strips
1 heaped teaspoon chopped fresh sage or
   ½ teaspoon dried sage
freshly ground black pepper
For the sauce
50 g/2 oz frozen apple slices, chopped
1 clove garlic, crushed
1 chicken stock cube
120 ml/4 fl oz dry cider

1   Slice the steaks lengthwise three-quarters of the way through the meat. Carefully open out and flatten.

2   Beat with a rolling pin so that the pork is an even thickness then sprinkle over half of the onion slices, the prunes, sage and black pepper.

3   Carefully roll up each piece of meat like a Swiss roll and secure with wooden cocktail sticks or string. Cut each roll in half.

4   Then make the sauce. Put the remaining onions in a dish with the apple and garlic, crumble in the chicken stock cube then pour in the cider.

5   Cook on HIGH for 4 minutes, then add the pork to the sauce. Cover with cling film and pierce. Cook for a further 4 minutes.

6   Cook on MEDIUM for 6-7 minutes or until the pork feels tender and the juices run clear when pierced with a sharp knife. Leave to STAND for 2 minutes.

7   Carefully remove the cocktail sticks or string and place the pork rolls on a warmed serving plate. Keep hot while you finish the sauce.

8   Taste the sauce and adjust the seasoning. Spoon a little over the meat then pour the remainder into a hot serving dish.

To freeze: allow to cool fully, then pack in a rigid container and label. Use within 1 month. Thaw for 10 minutes on DEFROST. Reheat on HIGH for 5-10 minutes or until piping hot.

Fibre	o	**Sugar**	o
Fat	o o	**Salt**	o o

Farmhouse turkey in wine and mustard sauce

Serves 4
450 g/1 lb frozen diced turkey, defrosted
4 rashers frozen back bacon, rinded and
   chopped
25 g/1 oz wholemeal flour
freshly ground black pepper
250 ml/8 fl oz white wine, e.g. Laski Riesling
175 g/6 oz frozen Stewpack, or an
   equivalent weight of fresh root vegetables,
   including swedes, carrots, turnips, onion
   and celery, peeled and diced
50 g/2 oz frozen whole small onions
2 tablespoons mild wholegrain mustard
1 chicken stock cube, crumbled

1   Place the turkey and bacon in a plastic bag with the flour and black pepper and shake until the meat is completely coated.

2   Pour the wine into a large serving dish, stir in the vegetables, mustard and stock cube. Stir well.

3   Cook uncovered on HIGH for 5 minutes or until the wine is boiling vigorously. Stir in the meat. Cover the dish with cling film, pierce, and cook for a further 5 minutes.

4   Cook on DEFROST for 10 minutes or until the vegetables are tender.

To freeze: cool, then pack into a rigid container. Seal and label. Use within 1 month. Thaw on DEFROST for 20 minutes in a covered serving dish, stirring occasionally to break down the block. Reheat on HIGH for 10-15 minutes or until piping hot.

Fibre	o o	**Sugar**	o
Fat	o	**Salt**	o o

Rogan Josh

Rogan josh

Serves 4
820 g/1 lb 12 oz can tomatoes, mashed
100 g/4 oz red lentils
175 g/6 oz frozen onion slices, or 2 small
   fresh onions, peeled and sliced
2-3 cloves garlic, crushed
2 tablespoons hot Madras curry powder
1 beef stock cube
450 g/1 lb frozen boneless lamb leg steaks,
   defrosted and cubed
2 tablespoons chopped fresh coriander
fresh coriander, to garnish

1 Place the tomatoes, lentils, onion, garlic, curry powder and stock cube in a bowl. Cover with cling film, pierce, and cook on HIGH for 25 minutes, stirring once.

2 Place the meat in a large bowl. Cook uncovered on HIGH for 2½ minutes, stir, then cook for a further 2½ minutes.

3 Toss the meat with the fresh coriander, then mix into the lentil mixture. Cook on MEDIUM for 15 minutes, or until the meat is tender. Garnish with coriander.

To freeze: cool, then pack into a rigid container: use within 2 months. Thaw on DEFROST for 15 minutes, then reheat on MEDIUM for 10-15 minutes or until hot.

| Fibre | ● ● | Sugar | ● |
| Fat | ● ● | Salt | ● ● |

Shredded beef with ginger

Serves 4

150 g/5 oz frozen lean fillet or rump steak,
*   partially defrosted and cut into thin strips*
2 teaspoons arrowroot or cornflour
1 teaspoon soft brown sugar
½-1 teaspoon ground ginger
¼ teaspoon five spice powder
1½-2 tablespoons soy sauce
4 tablespoons water
1 clove garlic, crushed
50 g/2 oz sliced mushrooms
100 g/4 oz green pepper, cored, seeded and
*   cut into matchstick strips*
100 g/4 oz frozen mange tout peas
5 spring onions, halved lengthways and cut
*   into 5 cm/2 inch lengths*

1 Put the beef in a plastic bag with the arrowroot or cornflour, sugar, ginger and five spice powder, then shake until the meat is completely coated.

2 Mix together the soy sauce, water and garlic in a large bowl. Stir in the beef mixture, then the mushrooms and green peppers. Half cover the bowl with cling film, pierce, then cook on HIGH for 3 minutes.

3 Stir well. Add the mange tout peas and spring onions then cook for a further 3 minutes. Stir once during the cooking time.

4 Serve with Brown rice (page 32) and other Chinese style dishes such as Sweet and sour vegetables with cashew nuts (page 33).

To freeze: not suitable for freezing.

Note: when cutting meat into very thin slices, it is easier to do so while the meat is still partially frozen.

| Fibre | ○ | Sugar | ○ ○ |
| Fat | ○ | Salt | ○ ○ |

Shredded beef with ginger

Autumn marrow

Serves 4
1 marrow, weighing about 1 kg/2 lb
40 g/1 ½ oz split red lentils
4 tablespoons hot water
1 clove garlic, crushed
100 g/4 oz frozen onion slices or 1 small
*   fresh onion, peeled and sliced*
175 g/6 oz frozen minced beef steak
2 tablespoons fresh wholemeal
*   breadcrumbs*
2 tablespoons tomato purée
1 tablespoon Worcestershire sauce
2 teaspoons chopped fresh thyme or
*   1 teaspoon dried thyme*
½ teaspoon yeast extract
freshly ground black pepper

1   Cut the marrow in half lengthways. Scoop out and discard all the seeds. Then scoop out the marrow flesh, leaving an even 1 cm/½ inch layer all around the marrow shell. Set aside the marrow. Chop the scooped out flesh and set aside.

2   Place the lentils in a bowl with the water. Cover with cling film and pierce. Cook on HIGH for 3 minutes, stirring halfway through cooking. Leave to STAND.

3   Place the garlic, onion and beef in a bowl. Cover with cling film, pierce, and cook on HIGH for 8 minutes, stirring halfway through cooking. Add the lentils, chopped marrow flesh and all the remaining ingredients. Mix well.

4   Place one marrow shell in a shallow serving dish. Pile the filling inside it and place the other half of the marrow on top. Secure with 4 cocktail sticks down each side. Cover with cling film and cook on HIGH for 10 minutes.

5   Cover with foil and leave to STAND for 6 minutes, then cut into slices and serve immediately.

To freeze: not suitable for freezing.

Fibre	● ●	Sugar	
Fat	●	Salt	●

Liver rissoles in spicy sauce

Serves 4-6
100 g/4 oz wholemeal bread
100 g/4 oz frozen onion slices, coarsely
*   chopped, or 1 small fresh onion, peeled*
*   and coarsely chopped*
225 g/8 oz frozen lambs' liver, defrosted
1 teaspoon finely chopped fresh sage, or
*   ½ teaspoon dried sage*
1 teaspoon Worcestershire sauce
1 egg
freshly ground black pepper
For the sauce
397 g/14 oz can tomatoes
2 teaspoons finely chopped fresh sage, or
*   1 teaspoon dried sage*
1 teaspoon Worcestershire sauce

1   Put the bread into a food processor or blender and process to make into crumbs. Add the remaining ingredients, season with black pepper to taste and process until well mixed.

2   Divide the mixture into 8 and make each portion into a ball. Arrange them in a circle on a large plate. Cook on HIGH for 3 minutes. Leave to STAND while making the sauce.

3   Process all the sauce ingredients. Pour into a bowl. Cover with cling film, pierce, and cook on HIGH for 2 minutes.

4   Add the rissoles to the sauce, cover again and cook on HIGH for a further 1½ minutes.

5   Serve the liver rissoles in spicy sauce with green noodles or mashed potatoes.

To freeze: pour the uncooked sauce straight over the rissoles and cover with cling film. Use within 3 months. To thaw and reheat pierce the cling film and thaw on DEFROST for 5 minutes, then cook in a serving dish on HIGH for a further 10 minutes.

Fibre	● ●	Sugar	●
Fat	● ●	Salt	● ●

Rosemary lamb

Serves 4

8 frozen best end of neck lamb cutlets,
   defrosted, fat removed
2 cloves garlic, crushed
2 tablespoons light soy sauce
2 tablespoons honey
1 teaspoon red wine vinegar
3 sprigs fresh rosemary, or 2 teaspoons
   dried rosemary
freshly ground black pepper
1 teaspoon wholemeal flour

1   Place the lamb cutlets in a large shallow
    dish. Mix together the garlic, soy sauce,
honey and wine vinegar. Brush the mixture
over the cutlets.

2   Break up the sprigs of rosemary and
    sprinkle over the lamb. Season with
freshly ground black pepper. Cover and
leave to marinate for 1 hour or more.

3   Pierce the cling film and cook on HIGH
    for 3 minutes. Drain the meat juices into
a small bowl, skim and reserve. Turn the
cutlets over, cover again and cook on HIGH
for a further 3 minutes.

4   Arrange the lamb cutlets on a hot
    serving plate and keep warm. Drain any
meat juices into the small bowl.

5   Blend the flour with a little cold water,
    add to the meat juices and cook on
HIGH for 1-2 minutes or until thickened,
stirring every 30 seconds to ensure a smooth
result.

6   Pour the gravy over the lamb cutlets and
    serve with a selection of freshly cooked
vegetables, including carrots, broad beans
and new potatoes.

To freeze: not suitable for freezing.

Note: if possible, leave the lamb to marinate
for about 6 hours or overnight, as this will
tenderize the meat and enhance its flavour.

Fibre	•	Sugar	• •
Fat	• •	Salt	• •

Lamb, coriander and courgette kebabs

Serves 4

450 g/1 lb frozen lamb leg steaks, defrosted
   and cubed
2 courgettes, about 75 g/3 oz each
12 frozen baby onions
For the marinade
1 teaspoon coriander seeds, crushed
2 cloves garlic, crushed
1 teaspoon paprika
2 tablespoons lemon juice
For the sauce
4 tablespoons thick set natural yogurt
2 teaspoons chopped fresh mint,
   or 1 teaspoon dried mint
freshly ground black pepper
1 large clove garlic, crushed

1   First mix together all the marinade
    ingredients. Stir the lamb into the
marinade and leave to stand for at least 1
hour so that the flavours penetrate the meat.

2   Score down the length of the
    courgettes with a potato peeler then cut
each courgette into eight thick slices.

3   Put the courgettes and onions into a
    bowl, cover with cling film, pierce, and
cook on HIGH for 2½ minutes to soften.

4   Thread the lamb, courgettes and onions
    on to wooden kebab sticks alternating
the foods as you thread them, then arrange
on a plate.

5   Cover with paper towels, then cook on
    HIGH for 2½ minutes. Turn over and
rearrange the kebabs so that the ones in the
middle are on the outside. Pour off the meat
juices and reserve. Cook the kebabs for a
further 2½ minutes.

6   Meanwhile mix the yogurt with the fresh
    mint, black pepper and garlic. Stir in a
little of the juices to make a smooth sauce.

To freeze: not suitable for freezing.

Fibre	•	Sugar	•
Fat	• •	Salt	•

Lamb and mushroom pilau

Serves 4
225 g/8 oz frozen diced lamb, defrosted
100 g/4 oz frozen sliced onions, or 1 small
   fresh onion, peeled and sliced
100 g/4 oz frozen peas
2 cloves garlic, crushed
1 teaspoon finely chopped root ginger
1 teaspoon garam masala
5 green cardamom pods (optional)
175 g/6 oz long grain brown rice
175 g/6 oz button mushrooms, sliced
1 teaspoon cayenne pepper

1   Place all the ingredients except the rice, mushrooms and cayenne pepper in a large bowl. Cover with cling film, pierce, and cook on HIGH for 5 minutes. Leave to STAND while cooking the rice.

2   Put the rice in a 1.75 litre/3 pint bowl. Pour over 450 ml/¾ pint boiling water. Cover with cling film, pierce, and cook on HIGH for 10 minutes. Stir and add 65 ml/ 2½ fl oz boiling water. Cover again and cook on HIGH for a further 5 minutes.

3   Add the meat mixture. Cover again and cook on HIGH for a further 5 minutes, stirring in the mushrooms after 2½ minutes.

4   Spoon the lamb and mushroom pilau on to a hot serving dish, sprinkle with cayenne pepper and serve with Spinach, cauliflower and courgette bhaji (page 38) and Spiced lentil dhal (page 39).

To freeze: this mixture can be divided between 4 individual plates, covered with a double layer of cling film and frozen. To reheat from frozen: pierce the cling film and cook each plate on HIGH for 5-6 minutes.

Variation
Omit the meat and stir in 225 g/8 oz frozen prawns for the last 5 minutes of cooking.

Fibre	● ●	Sugar	●
Fat	●	Salt	●

Glazed lamb with apricots

Serves 6
6 frozen lean double lamb chops, defrosted
   and trimmed of fat
2 teaspoons dark soy sauce
freshly ground black pepper
75 g/3 oz frozen mixed sliced peppers
2 tablespoons honey
2 tablespoons white wine vinegar
1 teaspoon made English mustard
285 g/10.5 oz can apricot halves in natural
   fruit juice

1   Brush the chops on both sides with the soy sauce. Arrange on a large plate and season with black pepper. Cover with cling film, pierce, and cook on MEDIUM for 4 minutes.

2   Drain off the fatty juices and turn the chops over; cover again and cook on MEDIUM for a further 3 minutes. Keep covered and leave to STAND.

3   Place the mixed peppers, honey, white wine vinegar, mustard and the juice from the can of apricots in a medium sized bowl. Cover with cling film, pierce, and cook on HIGH for 3 minutes. Stir once during the cooking period.

4   Slice the apricot halves and add to the sauce. Cover again and cook on HIGH for a further 1 minute or until the sauce is piping hot.

5   Pour the sauce over the chops. Return to the microwave cooker and cook the lamb chops on HIGH for 1-2 minutes to reheat if necessary.

6   Serve with new potatoes and a green vegetable, such as broad beans, peas or courgettes.

To freeze: not suitable for freezing.

Fibre	●	Sugar	● ●
Fat	●	Salt	●

Opposite *Glazed lamb with apricots*

HEALTHY FISH AND SHELLFISH

Fish and shellfish are among nature's healthiest foods. They are low in fat, high in protein, and rich in minerals – which makes them ideal foods to include in a healthy diet. The wealth of frozen fish and shellfish available nowadays means, too, that freshness need no longer be a problem. The recipes that follow are as beautiful to look at as they are light and tasty to eat. And they provide proof that, of all foods, fish is perhaps that best suited to microwave cooking.

Creamy smoked haddock pâté

Serves 4
225 g/8 oz frozen smoked haddock fillets,
*   skinned (see* **Note***) then defrosted*
175 g/6 oz low fat soft cheese
1 tablespoon lemon juice
freshly ground black pepper
4 tablespoons chopped fresh chives or
*   spring onion tops*

1   Arrange the haddock fillets on a dish with the tail ends towards the centre. Cover with cling film, pierce, and cook on HIGH for 3 minutes. Allow to STAND for 5 minutes.

2   Flake the fish into a medium bowl, removing any bones, then add the cheese, lemon juice, pepper and 3 tablespoons of the chives or spring onion tops. Beat together until well blended. Taste and add extra lemon juice, pepper, chives or spring onion tops if necessary. Beat again.

3   Spoon into a small serving dish then sprinkle the remaining 1 tablespoon of chives or spring onion tops around the edge to make an attractive border. Chill until required.

4   Serve the smoked haddock pâté as a starter with wholemeal or granary toast, or use in Wholemeal baps (page 42) with a salad for a packed lunch.

To freeze: overwrap with cling film and label. Use within 1 month. Thaw for 2 hours at room temperature.

Note: the fish is easily skinned while still lightly frozen: loosen from one corner and then tear the skin off.

| Fibre | ● | Sugar | |
| Fat | ● ● | Salt | ● ● ● |

Fish, tomato and walnut salad

Serves 4
225 g/8 oz potatoes, peeled or scraped, and
*   cut into 5 mm/¼ inch cubes*
1 frozen cod fillet, defrosted and cut into
*   cubes*
1 frozen smoked haddock fillet, defrosted
*   and cut into cubes*
2 tablespoons lemon juice
50 g/2 oz frozen whole small onions
2 tomatoes, skinned, each one cut into eight
*   wedges*
25 g/1 oz walnut pieces
150 ml/¼ pint cold Piquant sauce (page 23)
1 tablespoon chopped fresh parsley
1 red-skinned apple

1   Place the potatoes in a medium-sized bowl with 2 tablespoons of water. Cover with cling film, pierce, and cook on HIGH for 4 minutes. Drain, then transfer to a serving dish.

2 Place the cubed fish, 1 tablespoon of the lemon juice and onions in a bowl. Cover with cling film, pierce, and cook on HIGH for 3 minutes, stirring carefully halfway through the cooking time. Drain and add to the potatoes in the serving dish. Leave until cold.

3 Add the tomato and walnut pieces to the potato and fish mixture. Spoon the sauce on top then stir in carefully. Sprinkle with parsley.

4 Core the apple but do not peel. Slice thinly then toss in the remaining lemon juice to prevent discoloration. Arrange the slices, overlapping, round the edge of the dish.

To freeze: not suitable for freezing.

Note: this recipe can be served as a refreshing starter or as a main course salad. It could also be taken on a picnic.

Variation
Add a little tomato purée, a few finely chopped gherkins or a few capers to the Piquant sauce.

| Fibre | ○ | Sugar | ○ |
| Fat | ○ | Salt | ○ ○ |

Salmon with piquant tomato sauce

Serves 4
*4 frozen salmon steaks, about 175 g/6 oz each, defrosted (see **Note**)*
2 tablespoons white wine or water
4 bay leaves
freshly ground black pepper
For the sauce
knob of butter
2 teaspoons tomato purée
150 ml/¼ pint Piquant sauce (p 23)
1 tomato, skinned, seeded and finely chopped
2 tablespoons chopped fresh dill or parsley, or 1 tablespoon of dried dill
sprigs of fresh dill or parsley, to garnish

1 Arrange the salmon steaks in a shallow dish with the thin ends of the steaks to the centre. Add the wine or water and place a bay leaf on each steak. Season with pepper.

2 Cover with cling film, pierce, and cook on MEDIUM for 8-10 minutes, rearranging the fish after 6 minutes. Leave to STAND for 3 minutes.

3 Add the butter and tomato purée to the sauce. Cook on MEDIUM for 1 minute. Add the tomato and dill or parsley. Cook on MEDIUM for a further minute or until the sauce is hot.

4 Place the salmon steaks on a warmed serving plate. Spoon a little sauce over each piece of salmon and serve the remainder separately. Garnish with the sprigs of dill or parsley.

5 Serve the fish with a refreshing green salad made with oak leaf lettuce, lamb's lettuce and sprigs of dill. Alternatively serve with new potatoes and fennel or Julienne of vegetables (page 36).

To freeze: not suitable for freezing.

Notes: extra care should be taken when thawing salmon in the microwave cooker as it can easily begin to cook. Place the frozen steaks, thin ends towards the centre, in a shallow dish. Cover with cling film, pierce, and thaw on DEFROST for 10 minutes, turning halfway through the thawing time. Leave to STAND for 10-15 minutes. Alternatively thaw the salmon in the refrigerator.
Care should also be taken when cooking the fish as it is easily overcooked. Remove when it is just beginning to flake.

Variation
Trout can be substituted for the salmon steaks. Use one 175 g/6 oz trout per person. Alternatively use an equivalent weight of a non-oily white fish, such as cod, haddock, plaice or sole.

| Fibre | ○ | Sugar | ○ |
| Fat | ○ ○ ○ | Salt | ○ |

Colourful kebabs

Serves 4

*4 frozen smoked haddock fillets, skinned,
    defrosted and quartered*
*2 large courgettes, trimmed with a cannelle
    knife or potato peeler and cut into 24 slices*
24 frozen button mushrooms, defrosted
1 tablespoon grapeseed or vegetable oil
1 tablespoon white wine vinegar
*1 teaspoon chopped fresh thyme or
    ½ teaspoon dried thyme*
freshly ground black pepper
To garnish
½ lemon, cut into 8 wedges
sprigs of watercress

1 Thread the fish, courgette slices and mushrooms on to 8 bamboo skewers, alternating the various ingredients as you thread them.

2 Mix the oil and vinegar together, then brush the mixture over the kebabs. Finally, sprinkle them with the thyme and pepper.

3 Place the kebabs on a large plate and cover with absorbent kitchen paper. Cook on HIGH for 6 minutes, turning and brushing the kebabs with their cooking juices halfway through cooking.

4 Garnish with the lemon wedges and watercress and serve with Brown rice (page 32) or green noodles.

To freeze: not suitable for freezing.

Notes: take care not to overcook the fish. Grapeseed oil is a useful ingredient for healthy cooking as it contains virtually no cholesterol.

Variation
Cod or halibut can be used instead of smoked haddock.

| Fibre | • | Sugar | • |
| Fat | • | Salt | • |

Colourful kebabs

Salmon with piquant tomato sauce (page 21)

Piquant sauce

Makes 450 ml/¾ pint
275 ml/½ pint chicken or vegetable stock
1 teaspoon white wine vinegar
2 tablespoons lemon juice
2 eggs
1 tablespoon cornflour
1 teaspoon mustard powder
freshly ground black pepper
2 tablespoons natural yogurt

1   Put all the ingredients except the natural yogurt into a blender or food processor and process until smooth and well blended. Pour into a large bowl.

2   Cook on HIGH for 4 minutes, whisking 2 or 3 times during the cooking time. Add the yogurt and whisk well.

To freeze: pour into 3 small pots, leaving 2.5 cm/1 inch headspace. Use within 1 month. Thaw 1 pot at a time. Remove lid and thaw on DEFROST for 2 minutes. Turn into a bowl, whisk and thaw on DEFROST for a further 2 minutes, whisking once more.

Note: this sauce can be used with hot or cold dishes.

| Fibre | ● ● | Sugar | |
| Fat | ● | Salt | ● |

Plaice rolls with spinach and orange

Serves 4
4 frozen plaice fillets, skinned
then defrosted
For the stuffing
350 g/12 oz frozen chopped spinach,
defrosted
4 tablespoons frozen onion slices, or 1 small
fresh onion, peeled and sliced
grated rind of 1 orange
8 tablespoons fresh wholemeal
breadcrumbs
freshly ground black pepper
15 g/½ oz butter

1 Arrange the plaice fillets on a board, skinned side up.

2 Put the spinach, onion and half the orange rind in a bowl. Cover with cling film, pierce, and cook on HIGH for 3 minutes. Add breadcrumbs and season with pepper.

3 Divide the stuffing between the plaice fillets then roll them up like Swiss rolls from the wide end. Arrange the rolls in a circle in a shallow dish. Cover with cling film, pierce, and cook on HIGH for 6 minutes.

4 Put the butter and remaining orange rind in a small bowl. Cook on HIGH for 30 seconds, then brush over the plaice fillets before serving.

5 Arrange the rolls on a warmed serving dish and serve immediately with a vegetable accompaniment, such as Mushrooms and onions à la grecque (page 40) or Layered potato and apple bake (page 32).

To freeze: not suitable for freezing.

Note: for a special occasion meal, try using lemon sole fillets instead of the plaice fillets. Cook the lemon sole for 4 minutes on HIGH and proceed with steps 3 and 4 as above. If preferred, use the grated rind of 1 lemon in place of the orange rind.

Fibre	● ● ●	Sugar	●
Fat	●	Salt	●

Rainbow trout with watercress and almonds

Serves 2
2 frozen rainbow trout, about 225 g/8 oz
each, defrosted
100 g/4 oz frozen onion slices, or 1 small
fresh onion, peeled and sliced
50 g/2 oz watercress, roughly chopped
freshly ground black pepper
25 g/1 oz flaked almonds, toasted and
roughly chopped
¼ teaspoon grated lemon rind
1 tablespoon lemon juice
To garnish
flaked almonds, toasted
sprigs of watercress

1 Cut the fish along the back down to the spine. Carefully cut through the spine of the trout at the head and tail of the fish then very carefully ease the spine and bones away from the flesh and discard.

2 Place the onion, watercress and plenty of black pepper in a bowl. Cook uncovered on HIGH for 5 minutes. Add the almonds and lemon rind and mix well.

3 Use the watercress mixture to stuff the body cavities of the fish. Arrange the fish, head-to-tail, on a serving dish.

4 Pour the lemon juice over the fish. Season with more black pepper then cover with cling film, pierce, and cook on MEDIUM for 7-8 minutes or until the fish flakes easily when tested with a knife.

5 Garnish with the toasted flaked almonds and sprigs of watercress. Serve immediately with new potatoes and green vegetables or a side salad.

To freeze: not suitable for freezing.

Note: if watercress is not available use 50 g/2 oz frozen chopped spinach, defrosted and drained, in the recipe, and garnish with sprigs of parsley.

Fibre	● ●	Sugar	●
Fat	● ●	Salt	●

Paprika prawns with tomato and pasta

Serves 2-3
100 g/4 oz small wholemeal pasta shapes
900 ml/1 ½ pints boiling water
For the sauce
100 g/4 oz frozen onion slices or 1 small
*   fresh onion, peeled and sliced*
2 cloves garlic, crushed
2 tomatoes, skinned and roughly chopped
¼ teaspoon paprika
1 tablespoon tomato purée
freshly ground black pepper
100 g/4 oz frozen peeled prawns
1 tablespoon chopped fresh chives, basil or
*   parsley, to serve*

1   Place the pasta in a 2.25 litre/4 pint bowl. Pour over the boiling water, then cover with cling film and pierce. Cook on HIGH for 5 minutes or until the pasta is just chewy, then leave to stand to complete cooking, while making the sauce.

2   Place the onion, garlic, tomatoes, paprika and tomato purée in a bowl then season generously with black pepper. Cover with cling film, pierce, and cook on HIGH for 4 minutes.

3   Stir in the frozen prawns and cover again. Cook for a further 2-3 minutes or until the prawns are thawed and heated through. The onions should be tender.

4   Drain the pasta and season with more black pepper. Toss the fresh herbs into the pasta then transfer immediately to a hot serving dish.

5   Spoon the prawn mixture over the pasta and serve immediately with a mixed salad.

To freeze: not suitable for freezing

Note: to save time, the pasta can be boiled conventionally while the sauce is being prepared in the microwave cooker.

Fibre	● ● ●	Sugar	●
Fat	●	Salt	●

Middle eastern cod with prawns

Serves 4
75 g/3 oz frozen onion slices, or 1 small fresh
*   onion, peeled and sliced*
¼ teaspoon ground turmeric
¼ teaspoon ground paprika
¼ teaspoon ground allspice
¼ teaspoon ground nutmeg
freshly ground black pepper
4 large tomatoes, roughly chopped
6 stuffed olives, halved
4 × 75 g/3 oz frozen cod steaks, defrosted
100 g/4 oz frozen peeled prawns, defrosted
To garnish
1 tablespoon chopped fresh coriander
lemon wedges

1   Place the onion slices in a bowl and sprinkle over the turmeric, paprika, allspice and nutmeg. Season with freshly ground black pepper. Cover with cling film, pierce, and cook on HIGH for 5 minutes or until the onion slices are soft and the spices will blended.

2   Mix the tomatoes and olives into the cooked onion mixture. Transfer to a serving dish and place the cod steaks on top, ensuring that the thin ends of the fish point towards the middle of the dish. Cover again, pierce, and cook on HIGH for a further 4 minutes.

3   Rearrange the fish and sprinkle over the prawns. Cook on HIGH for 1-2 more minutes, then garnish with the chopped fresh coriander and lemon wedges.

4   Serve with crisp, cooked vegetables and new potatoes, or brown rice mixed with toasted flaked almonds and 1 tablespoon of sultanas.

To freeze: not suitable for freezing.

Variation
Substitute frozen haddock steaks for the cod steaks, and garnish with mint instead of coriander.

Fibre	●	Sugar	●
Fat		Salt	●

Sole and smoked salmon rolls

Serves 8 as a starter
4 frozen lemon sole fillets, defrosted
100 g/4 oz frozen smoked salmon slices,
 defrosted and cut into 8 strips
4 tablespoons white wine
1 tablespoon cornflour
85 ml/3 fl oz skimmed milk
15 g/½ oz butter
freshly ground white pepper
1 tablespoon chopped fresh chives
1 teaspoon lemon juice
1 tablespoon chopped fresh parsley

1 Cut each fillet down the centre with sharp scissors to obtain 8 long strips of fish.

2 Place a strip of smoked salmon on the skin side of each piece of fish. Roll up the fish from its widest end like a Swiss roll, and secure with a wooden cocktail stick.

3 Arrange the fish rolls, spiral ends upwards, around the edge of a 20 cm/ 8 inch dish. Pour over the wine. Cover with cling film, pierce, and cook on HIGH for 3 minutes.

4 Pour the cooking liquid into a large bowl and blend with the cornflour and milk. Add the butter and pepper then cook on HIGH for 4 minutes or until thickened, stirring once during the cooking time. Add the chives, lemon juice and parsley then cook for a further 1 minute.

5 Arrange the fish rolls on a warmed serving dish. Pour the sauce round the fish and serve immediately.

To freeze: not suitable for freezing.

Notes: this dish can be made with plaice fillets. If skinned fillets are preferred, remove the skin while the fish is still slightly frozen as the skin can be removed more easily, then proceed as above with the recipe. This dish can be served as a main course for 4.

Fibre	○	**Sugar**	○
Fat	○ ○	**Salt**	○ ○

Centre *Sole and smoked salmon rolls; Scallops and prawns with Pernod (page 28)*

Scallops and prawns with Pernod

Serves 4 as a starter
100 g/4 oz frozen prawns
100 g/4 oz frozen scallops
1 teaspoon lemon juice
1 clove garlic, crushed
1 teaspoon chopped mixed fresh herbs, or a
* pinch of mixed dried herbs*
15 g/½ oz butter
1 large carrot, peeled
5 cm/2 inch piece of cucumber
2 tablespoons Pernod
2 teaspoons arrowroot
freshly ground black pepper
1 tablespoon chopped fresh parsley

1 Place the prawns, scallops, lemon juice, garlic, herbs and butter in a medium bowl. Cover with cling film, pierce, and cook on MEDIUM for 3 minutes.

2 Cut the carrot and cucumber into thin matchstick strips. Place in a small bowl with the Pernod. Cover with cling film, pierce, and cook on MEDIUM for 2 minutes.

3 Spoon the carrot and cucumber mixture into scallop shells or small dishes, reserving the cooking liquid. Spoon the prawns and scallops on top, reserving the cooking liquid.

4 Blend the arrowroot with a little water in a medium-sized bowl. Combine the reserved juices and whisk them into the blended arrowroot. Cook on HIGH for 1½ minutes, whisking after 1 minute.

5 Spoon the sauce over the seafood and vegetables. Place the dishes in the microwave cooker and cook on HIGH for ½-1 minute or until hot.

6 Sprinkle with black pepper and parsley. Serve immediately with small crusty wholemeal rolls.

To freeze: not suitable for freezing.

| Fibre | ◦ | Sugar | ◦ |
| Fat | ◦ | Salt | ◦ |

Provençale tuna lasagne

Serves 4-6
450 g/1 lb frozen Ratatouille Mix, or an
* equivalent weight of fresh vegetables,*
* including tomatoes, aubergines,*
* courgettes, peppers and onions, trimmed*
* and diced*
400 g/14 oz can peeled tomatoes
2 cloves garlic, crushed
1-1½ teaspoons dried basil
198 g/7 oz can tuna fish in brine, drained
2 frozen cod or haddock steaks, about
* 75 g/3 oz each, defrosted and cut into*
* chunks*
freshly ground black pepper
9 sheets lasagne verdi
For the sauce
50 g/2 oz wholemeal flour
25 g/1 oz butter, chopped
600 ml/1 pint skimmed milk
freshly ground black pepper
100 g/4 oz Gouda or Edam, grated

1 Place the Ratatouille Mix or fresh vegetables in a large bowl. If using fresh vegetables add 4 tablespoons of water. Cover with cling film, pierce, and cook on HIGH for 5 minutes or until softened. Fresh vegetables may take slightly longer to soften. Drain off the excess liquid and reserve.

2 Stir in the tomatoes, garlic, basil, tuna and cod or haddock then season with freshly ground black pepper. Add 1-2 tablespoons of the ratatouille liquid to moisten.

3 Place three sheets of lasagne on the base of a 20×25 cm/8×10 inch deep serving dish, in a single layer.

4 Spoon over half the ratatouille and fish mixture, cover with three more sheets of lasagne then spoon over the remaining mixture.

5 To make the sauce, place the flour, butter, milk and black pepper in a large bowl. Heat uncovered on HIGH for 2 minutes. Whisk, then cook for a further 8 minutes whisking vigorously every 2 minutes.

6 Place the remaining lasagne on top of the ratatouille mixture. Add three-quarters of the cheese to the sauce then pour the sauce evenly into the dish so that the lasagne is completely covered.

7 Cover with cling film, pierce, and cook on HIGH for 15 minutes. STAND for 10 minutes.

8 Sprinkle over the remaining cheese and brown under a preheated hot grill before serving.

9 Eat with a crisp green salad or a crunchy apple and mint salad.

To freeze: cool completely then cover with 2 layers of cling film. Use within 1 month. To serve, pierce the cling film then thaw on DEFROST for 15-20 minutes. STAND for 15 minutes until completely thawed. Reheat on HIGH for about 15 minutes or until the centre of the lasagne is piping hot.

Fibre	• •	Sugar	•
Fat	• •	Salt	• • •

Haddock mornay

Serves 4
4× 75 g/3 oz frozen haddock steaks
juice of ½ small lemon
1 egg
300 ml/½ pint skimmed milk
25 g/1 oz Gruyère cheese, grated
freshly ground black pepper
3 tablespoons chopped fresh parsley

1 Place the steaks in a large shallow dish and sprinkle with the lemon juice. Cover with cling film, pierce, and cook on HIGH for 3 minutes.

2 Combine the remaining ingredients and pour over the fish. Cover again, pierce, and cook on HIGH for 6-8 minutes.

To freeze: not suitable for freezing

Fibre	•	Sugar	•
Fat	• •	Salt	• •

Mixed fish crumble

Serves 4
3× 75 g/3 oz frozen cod steaks, defrosted
225 g/8 oz frozen smoked mackerel fillets, defrosted
100 g/4 oz frozen onion slices or 1 small fresh onion, peeled and sliced
100 g/4 oz frozen Mexican Mix, or an equivalent weight of fresh vegetables including diced red and green peppers, sweetcorn and chopped onion
1 tablespoon lemon juice
2 tomatoes, skinned and chopped
25 g/1 oz gherkins, sliced
2 tablespoons tartare sauce
freshly ground black pepper
For the topping
50 g/2 oz fresh wholemeal breadcrumbs
25 g/1 oz natural wheatgerm
25 g/1 oz mature Cheddar cheese, grated

1 Place the cod on a plate and cover with cling film. Pierce and cook on MEDIUM for 4 minutes then flake.

2 Flake the smoked mackerel and discard the skin.

3 Combine the fish in a 1.5 litre/2½ pint dish with the onion and Mexican Mix. If using fresh vegetables, add 2 tablespoons water. Cover with cling film, pierce, and cook on HIGH for 5 minutes or until the vegetables have softened slightly.

4 Stir in the lemon juice, tomatoes and gherkins. Cover again and cook on HIGH for a further 2 minutes. Stir in the tartare sauce and season with pepper.

5 Sprinkle the breadcrumbs, wheatgerm and cheese on top of the mixed fish. Place under a preheated hot grill until brown.

To freeze: not suitable for freezing.

Variation
Any combination of white and oily fish can be used for this tasty, colourful dish.

Fibre	• •	Sugar	•
Fat	• •	Salt	• •

HEALTHY VEGETABLES, GRAINS, AND PULSES

Everyone agrees that meals made from vegetables, grains and pulses make a refreshing – and healthy – change once in a while.
These delicious, high fibre recipes will persuade you that once in a while is not enough; you'll want to eat them more often.
With the freezer and microwave cooker at your elbow to help, you can cook vegetables perfectly in a fraction of the time it would normally take. You'll find that healthy eating has never been so easy or so enjoyable!

Spring leaf parcels

Serves 4
8 medium-sized Savoy cabbage leaves
4 tablespoons boiling water
For the filling
225 g/8 oz dried butter beans
300 ml/1/2 pint cold water
900 ml/1 1/2 pints boiling water
100 g/4 oz frozen onion slices, or 1 small
  fresh onion, peeled and sliced
1 clove garlic, crushed
100 g/4 oz frozen sweetcorn
50 g/2 oz hazelnuts, toasted and chopped
1/2 teaspoon ground cinnamon
1/2 teaspoon ground allspice
1/4 teaspoon ground nutmeg
freshly ground black pepper
397 g/14 oz can tomatoes, drained and juice
  reserved

1 First cook the butter beans. Place the beans in a large bowl, and cover with 300 ml/1/2 pint cold water. Cover with cling film, pierce, and cook on HIGH for 10 minutes. Leave to STAND and swell for 1 1/2 hours.

2 Drain the beans and rinse in hot water. Place the beans in a large bowl and add 600 ml/1 pint boiling water. Cover with cling film, pierce, and cook on HIGH for 45-50 minutes, adding a further 300 ml/1/2 pint

boiling water halfway through the cooking time. Set aside.

3 Place 4 cabbage leaves in a large bowl with 4 tablespoons boiling water. Cover with cling film, pierce, and cook on HIGH for 3 minutes. Remove the blanched leaves and plunge into cold water. Place the remaining leaves in the bowl and blanch as before.

4 To make the filling, mix the onions, garlic, sweetcorn, hazelnuts, spices and seasoning in a medium bowl. Cover with cling film, pierce, and cook on HIGH for 5 minutes. Stir in the beans and tomatoes and cook on HIGH for 2 more minutes.

5 Divide the mixture equally between the 8 cabbage leaves and roll them up from the stalk end to form parcels. Pack them closely in a shallow dish join side down. Pour the reserved tomato juice over the parcels and season well. Cover with cling film, pierce, then cook on HIGH for 8 minutes.

To freeze: prepare the parcels to the final step. Cover with a double layer of cling film and freeze. Use within 3 months. To reheat from frozen, pierce the cling film then cook on HIGH for 15 minutes.

Fibre	● ● ●	Sugar	●
Fat	●	Salt	● ●

Top left *Spiced potatoes; Spring leaf parcels*

Spiced potatoes

Serves 4
450 g/1 lb unpeeled potatoes, diced
100 g/4 oz frozen onion slices, or 1 small
fresh onion, peeled and sliced
1-2 cloves garlic, crushed
3 tablespoons water
½ teaspoon turmeric
½ teaspoon cumin seeds
1 teaspoon yellow or black mustard seeds
freshly ground black pepper

1 Place the potatoes and onion in a serving dish.

2 Blend the garlic with the water, spices and pepper, then pour the spice mixture over the potatoes. Mix thoroughly until the potatoes are pale yellow.

3 Cover with cling film, pierce, and cook on HIGH for 5 minutes. Stir, cover again, then cook for a further 5 minutes or until the potatoes are almost tender. Leave to STAND for 2 minutes.

4 Serve the spiced potatoes hot or cold as part of an Indian-style meal, or as an accompaniment to fish or meat kebabs and vegetarian dishes.

To freeze: not suitable for freezing.

| Fibre | ● | Sugar | ● |
| Fat | | Salt | ● |

Perfect brown rice

Serves 4

225 g/8 oz American long grain brown rice
750 ml/1 1/4 pints boiling water
1/4 teaspoon sea salt (optional)

1 Put the rice into a 2.75 litre/5 pint bowl.
Pour over 600 ml/1 pint of the boiling water then stir in the salt, if using.

2 Cover with cling film, pierce, and cook on HIGH for 15 minutes.

3 Stir in the remaining boiling water, cover again, pierce, then cook for a further 15 minutes or until the rice is cooked and the water is absorbed.

4 Stir the rice thoroughly with a fork before serving. If serving rice with another dish that requires microwave cooking, e.g. a curry, cook the rice in advance and reheat in the microwave just before serving.

5 To reheat, add 2 tablespoons of water to the rice, cover with cling film, pierce, and reheat on HIGH for 3-4 minutes.

To freeze: cool then pack into a container. Use within 6 months. To reheat a serving for 4, turn the block into a serving dish, cover with cling film, pierce, and cook on HIGH for 10-15 minutes, breaking down the block as it thaws.

Variation

Brown rice to serve 3
Put 175 g/6 oz rice into a 1.75 litre/3 pint bowl with 450 ml/3/4 pint boiling water and salt, if using. Cover with cling film, pierce, and cook on HIGH for 12 minutes. Stir in 150 ml/1/4 pint more boiling water, cover again, then cook on HIGH for a further 12 minutes.

Brown rice to serve 2
Put 100 g/4 oz rice in 1.2 litre/2 pint bowl with 300 ml/1/2 pint boiling water and salt, if using. Cover with cling film, pierce, and cook on HIGH for 10 minutes. Add 150 ml/1/4 pint more boiling water, cover again, then cook for a further 10 minutes.

Brown rice to serve 1
Put 50 g/2 oz rice in a 1.2 litre/2 pint bowl with 250 ml/8 fl oz boiling water and salt if using. Cover with cling film, pierce, and cook on HIGH for 10 minutes. Stir in 50 ml/2 fl oz more boiling water, cover again, then cook for a further 5 minutes.

For Nutty tomato and coriander rice:
3 minutes before the end of the cooking time stir in 2 firm tomatoes, cut into wedges; 2 tablespoons each chopped fresh coriander and diced onion and 3 tablespoons toasted cashew nuts.

Note: the cooking times given above may vary slightly, depending on the type and origin of the long grain brown rice used. Adjust if necessary.

Fibre	• • •	Sugar
Fat	•	Salt • • •

Layered potato and apple bake

Serves 4

450 g/1 lb unpeeled potatoes, thinly sliced
100 g/4 oz frozen onion slices, or 1 fresh
leek, very finely sliced
50 g/2 oz frozen apple slices, chopped
2 cloves garlic, crushed
freshly ground black pepper
large pinch ground nutmeg
4 tablespoons vegetable stock or dry cider

For the topping
25 g/1 oz low fat Cheddar-type cheese,
grated
15 g/1/2 oz hazelnuts, chopped

1 Reserve a third of the potato slices then mix the remainder with the onion or leek, apple, garlic, black pepper and nutmeg.

2 Pile into a 1.2 litre/2 pint serving dish then arrange the reserved potato slices round the edge so they overlap.

3 Pour the stock or cider over the potatoes, cover with cling film and pierce. Cook on HIGH for 15 minutes or until the potatoes are just tender when tested with a knife. Leave to STAND for 5 minutes.

4 Sprinkle the cheese and hazelnuts over the potatoes then brown under a preheated hot grill. Serve immediately.

To freeze: cool, then overwrap with cling film. Use within 3 months. Thaw by piercing the cling film, then reheating on HIGH for about 10 minutes.

Note: this recipe is suitable as a vegetarian main meal for two. Use 75 g/3 oz cheese and 25 g/1 oz hazelnuts and serve with a crisp mixed salad.

Fibre	● ●	Sugar	●
Fat	●	Salt	●

Courgette twists

Serves 4 as an accompaniment
4 courgettes, weighing in total about 450 g/
   1 lb, trimmed
1 clove garlic, crushed
50 g/2 oz frozen mixed sliced peppers
2 teaspoons chopped fresh marjoram, or 1
   teaspoon dried marjoram
freshly ground black pepper
25 g/1 oz mature Cheddar cheese, grated
4 rashers frozen lean bacon, defrosted and
   rinded

1 Halve the courgettes lengthways. Hollow out the flesh from the centre with a teaspoon and roughly chop. Mix this in a bowl with the garlic, peppers, marjoram and seasoning. Cover with cling film, pierce, and cook on HIGH for 4 minutes.

2 Stir in the cheese. Pile the filling into the courgette halves and push the halves back together. Stretch each rasher of bacon with the blunt edge of a knife and wrap a rasher of bacon around each courgette. Secure the courgettes together with wooden cocktail sticks.

3 Place the courgettes in a shallow dish, cover with cling film, pierce, and cook on HIGH for 4 minutes. Rearrange the courgettes, cover again and cook on HIGH for a further 4 minutes. If liked, place the courgettes under a preheated hot grill to crisp the bacon.

To freeze: not suitable for freezing.

Note: this recipe can be served as a supper dish for two. If you wish, increase the weight of the cheese to 75 g/3 oz, and serve with baked tomatoes.

Fibre	● ●	Sugar	●
Fat	● ●	Salt	● ●

Sweet and sour vegetables with cashew nuts

Serves 4
227 g/8 oz can pineapple in natural juice, fruit
   chopped and juice reserved
2 teaspoons cornflour
1 tablespoon soy sauce
1½ tablespoons red wine vinegar
225 g/8 oz frozen Oriental Mix, or an
   equivalent weight of fresh vegetables,
   including bean sprouts, water chestnuts,
   sweetcorn, sliced mushrooms, sliced red
   peppers, sliced green beans and bamboo
   shoots
100 g/4 oz frozen mange tout peas
50 g/2 oz cashew nuts, toasted

1 Mix 3 tablespoons of the reserved pineapple juice with the soy sauce, cornflour and vinegar. Stir well then cook on HIGH for 2 minutes or until lightly thickened.

2 Stir in the remaining pineapple juice, then add the vegetables and chopped pineapple.

3 Cover with cling film, pierce, and cook on HIGH for 3 minutes. Stir then cook for a further 3 minutes or until the vegetables are just cooked and still crisp.

4 Toss the cashew nuts into the vegetables before serving. Serve with Brown rice (page 32) and a main dish such as Shredded beef with ginger (page 15).

To freeze: not suitable for freezing.

Fibre	● ●	Sugar	●
Fat	●	Salt	● ●

Lentil moussaka

Serves 4
100 g/4 oz dried red lentils
400 g/14 oz can tomatoes
1 clove garlic, crushed
1 teaspoon chopped fresh oregano, or
  ½ teaspoon dried oregano
ground nutmeg
1 vegetable stock cube
150 ml/¼ pint boiling water
225 g/8 oz aubergine, sliced
100 g/4 oz frozen onion slices, or 1 small
  fresh onion, peeled and chopped
For the cheese topping
1 egg
150 g/5 oz low fat soft cheese
freshly ground black pepper
a sprig of fresh marjoram, to garnish

1 Put the lentils in a 2.25 litre/4 pint bowl with the tomatoes, garlic, oregano and a generous pinch of nutmeg. Crumble in the stock cube then pour in the boiling water.

2 Stir well, cover with cling film, pierce, and cook on HIGH for 10 minutes.

3 Remove the lentil mixture and allow to STAND for 5 minutes.

4 Place the aubergine slices in a bowl with the onions. Cover with cling film, pierce, and cook on HIGH for 5 minutes.

5 Arrange half the aubergine slices and onion on the base of a 20 cm/8 inch round serving dish. Spoon over half the lentils then repeat the layers.

6 Cover with cling film, pierce, and cook on HIGH for 5 minutes.

7 Beat the egg into the cheese, then season with nutmeg and black pepper. Pour the cheese mixture over the lentil mixture and level the top. Cover again then cook on DEFROST for 4 minutes or until the cheese mixture has set.

8 Garnish the moussaka with sprigs of fresh marjoram placed at the edge of the dish. Serve immediately.

To freeze: not suitable for freezing.

| Fibre | ● ● ● | Sugar | ● |
| Fat | ● ● | Salt | ● ● |

Top left *Lentil moussaka;* **Bottom left** *Julienne of vegetables (page 36);*
Above right *Rosy cabbage with caraway and walnuts (page 36)*

Rosy cabbage with caraway and walnuts

Serves 6
450 g/1 lb red cabbage, shredded
1 tablespoon red wine vinegar
3 tablespoons pickled beetroot juice
½ teaspoon caraway seeds
2 teaspoons brown sugar
freshly ground black pepper
100 g/4 oz pickled beetroot, cut into strips
100 g/4 oz frozen onion slices, or 1 small
*   fresh onion, peeled and sliced*
100 g/4 oz frozen apple slices
2 tablespoons currants
25 g/1 oz walnut pieces, to garnish

1 Put the cabbage in a large bowl with the vinegar, beetroot juice, caraway seeds and sugar. Add plenty of black pepper then cover with cling film and pierce.

2 Cook on HIGH for 5 minutes. Stir well, mix in the remaining ingredients (except the walnuts), cover again then cook for a further 5 minutes or until the cabbage is tender, but still crisp. Garnish with the nuts.

3 Serve hot with a main course dish such as Liver rissoles in spicy sauce (page 16) or cold with salad.

To freeze: cool, then pack into a freezer bag and label. Use within 2 months. Thaw on DEFROST for 10 minutes, breaking down the block as it softens. Reheat if desired for 5 minutes on HIGH.

Fibre	● ●	Sugar	●
Fat	●	Salt	●

Julienne of vegetables

Serves 4
175 g/6 oz carrots, trimmed
3 sticks celery, trimmed
2 tablespoons water
175 g/6 oz frozen whole green beans
For the dressing
1 tablespoon walnut oil
1 teaspoon red wine vinegar
1 tablespoon sesame seeds, toasted

1 Cut the carrots and celery into 5 cm/ 2 inch long matchstick strips. Place the carrots in a shallow dish with the water. Cover with cling film, pierce, and cook on HIGH for 3 minutes.

2 Stir in the celery sticks and green beans. Cover again and cook on HIGH for 6 minutes, stirring halfway through the cooking time.

3 Drain off the liquid. Stir in the oil and vinegar, sprinkle with sesame seeds and cook on HIGH for 30 seconds.

4 Serve as a vegetable accompaniment to main course dishes.

To freeze: not suitable for freezing.

Note: these vegetables should be served *al dente* (crisp and firm). If you prefer them softer, then cook a few minutes longer before adding the dressing.

Variations
The three vegetables used in the recipe can be varied. Make potato or parsnip sticks, and add sticks of peppers, courgettes or spring onion.

Fibre	●	Sugar	●
Fat	● ●	Salt	●

Stilton and walnut stuffed onions

Serves 4
4 medium onions, about 175 g/6 oz each,
*   peeled*
2 tablespoons water
25 g/1 oz walnut pieces
25 g/1 oz dates, stoned and chopped
50 g/2 oz frozen apple slices, chopped
50 g/2 oz Stilton cheese, crumbled
freshly ground black pepper

1 Slice the roots and tops off the onions. Arrange the onions in a circle in a shallow dish and add the water. Cover with cling film, pierce, and cook on HIGH for 8 minutes. Leave to STAND for 2 minutes.

2 Drain off the liquid. Hollow out the centre of each onion with a teaspoon, leaving a 3 layer 'shell'. Chop the onion centres and mix with the walnut, date and apple pieces and half the cheese. Season well with black pepper.

3 Spoon this mixture into the onion shells. Spread any remaining mixture round the onions in the dish. Sprinkle with the remaining cheese. Cover again and cook on HIGH for a further 2 minutes.

4 Place the dish under a preheated hot grill until browned and bubbling.

5 Serve with grilled chops or cold meat and salad or with Spiced potatoes (page 31) for a vegetarian meal.

To freeze: not suitable for freezing.

Fibre	● ●	Sugar	●
Fat	● ●	Salt	● ● ●

Aubergine and potato timbale

Serves 4-6
225 g/8 oz potatoes, sliced thinly
2 tablespoons water
2 medium sized aubergines, sliced thinly
2 tablespoons olive oil
2 teaspoons chopped fresh marjoram, or
*   1 teaspoon dried marjoram*
300 ml/½ pint skimmed milk
2 large eggs

1 Place the potatoes in a bowl with the water. Cover with cling film, pierce, and cook on HIGH for 4 minutes or until the potatoes are just tender.

2 Heat a browning dish according to the manufacturer's instructions. Place half the aubergine slices in the heated dish and sprinkle with half the oil. Cover with cling film, pierce, and cook on HIGH for 5 minutes. Turn the aubergine slices and cook for a further 2 minutes on HIGH. Set the cooked aubergine aside and cook the remaining aubergine with the remaining oil in the microwave cooker as before.

3 Layer the aubergine slices in a 1 litre/ 1¾ pint soufflé dish. Sprinkle with the marjoram. Arrange the potato slices on top.

4 Beat the milk and eggs and strain over the potato layer. Season if liked. Cover with cling film, pierce, and cook on DEFROST for 16-18 minutes until the mixture is almost set. Leave to STAND for 5 minutes before serving.

To freeze: not suitable for freezing.

Fibre	● ●	Sugar	
Fat	● ●	Salt	

Broccoli parmigiani

Serves 4
450 g/1 lb frozen broccoli
300 ml/½ pint skimmed milk
25 g/1 oz wholemeal flour
15 g/½ oz butter
1 teaspoon wholegrain mustard
50 g/2 oz Parma ham, cut into thin strips
40 g/1½ oz Parmesan cheese, grated
freshly ground black pepper

1 Arrange the broccoli in a shallow serving dish. Cover with cling film, pierce, and cook on HIGH for 5 minutes. Drain if necessary. Set aside, covered.

2 Put the milk and flour into a medium bowl. Whisk well. Add the butter and mustard. Cook on HIGH for 5 minutes, whisking halfway through the cooking time.

3 Stir in the ham and half the cheese. Pour the sauce over the broccoli and sprinkle with the remaining cheese and plenty of freshly ground black pepper.

4 Cook uncovered, on HIGH for 4 minutes. Place the dish under a pre-heated hot grill to brown the top before serving.

To freeze: not suitable for freezing.

Fibre	● ●	Sugar	
Fat	●	Salt	●

Left *Spiced lentil dhal; Spinach, cauliflower and courgette bhaji*

Spinach, cauliflower and courgette bhaji

Serves 4
225 g/8 oz frozen leaf spinach
225 g/8 oz frozen cauliflower florets
225 g/8 oz frozen sliced courgettes
100 g/4 oz frozen onion slices, or 1 small
fresh onion, peeled and sliced
1 tablespoon water
2 cloves garlic, crushed
½ teaspoon grated or very finely chopped
fresh root ginger, or
¼ teaspoon ground ginger
1 teaspoon garam masala
1-2 teaspoons black mustard seeds
1-2 tablespoons thick set natural yogurt

1 Put the vegetables in a large bowl with the water, garlic and ginger. Cover with cling film, pierce, and cook on HIGH for 5 minutes.

2 Stir thoroughly then add the garam masala and mustard seeds. Cover again and cook for a further 10 minutes, or until the vegetables are just tender, stirring once during the cooking time.

3 Just before serving, stir the yogurt into the vegetables. Serve with Rogan josh (page 14) and Brown rice (page 32) or serve as a main course for two with rice and Spiced lentil dhal.

To freeze: not suitable for freezing

1 Place all the ingredients in a 2.25 litre/ 4 pint bowl. Cover with cling film and pierce.

2 Cook on HIGH for 15 minutes. Stir halfway through the cooking time and top up with a little boiling water, if necessary. The dhal should be thick and the lentils should be soft and still retain their shape.

3 Serve the dhal as an accompaniment to an Indian dish such as Tandoori-style chicken (page 12).

To freeze: cool, pack into a rigid container and label. Use within 3 months. Reheat from frozen on HIGH for 10-15 minutes.

Note: for a vegetarian main meal serve with the Spinach, cauliflower and courgette bhaji (left) and Brown rice (page 32).

Fibre	● ● ●	Sugar	●
Fat	●	Salt	●

Mushrooms and onions à la grecque (page 40)

Note: frozen broccoli can be used in place of the cauliflower, and frozen mixed sliced peppers in place of the courgettes.

Fibre	● ●	Sugar	●
Fat		Salt	●

Spiced lentil dhal

Serves 4-6

100 g/4 oz dried red lentils
225 g/8 oz frozen onion slices, or 2 small fresh onions, peeled and chopped
450 ml/¾ pint boiling chicken or vegetable stock
3 cloves garlic, crushed
½ teaspoon ground turmeric
1 teaspoon paprika
1 teaspoon ground coriander
1 teaspoon ground cumin

Mushrooms and onions à la grecque

Serves 6 as a starter
4 tablespoons red wine
1½ tablespoons red or white wine
  vinegar
3 tablespoons tomato purée
1 tablespoon olive oil
1 clove garlic, crushed
6 coriander seeds
6 black peppercorns
1 bay leaf
450 g/1 lb frozen whole mushrooms
225 g/8 oz frozen small whole onions
2 tablespoons chopped fresh parsley, to
  garnish

1 Whisk all the liquid ingredients together in a large bowl then add the remaining ingredients, except the parsley.

2 Cover with cling film, pierce, and cook on HIGH for 12 minutes, stirring twice during the cooking time.

3 Leave to cool, then chill before spooning into a serving dish. Taste and adjust the seasoning.

4 To garnish, sprinkle with parsley and serve immediately with hot crusty wholemeal bread rolls.

To freeze: Cool and pack in a rigid container, leaving 2.5 cm/1 inch headspace. Use within 1 month. To serve, remove lid. Thaw on DEFROST for 5 minutes, turn into a dish and cook on HIGH for 8 minutes, stirring occasionally until thawed but not hot.

Variations
Mushrooms and onions à la grecque can also be served hot, as a starter or vegetable accompaniment.
For Leeks and mushrooms à la grecque, substitute the button onions with 3 medium-sized leeks, washed and cut into 2.5 cm/1 inch lengths. Garnish with chives rather than parsley.

Fibre	● ●	Sugar	●
Fat	● ●	Salt	● ●

Barley bake

Serves 4
100 g/4 oz pearl barley
½ teaspoon fennel seeds
175 g/6 oz frozen onion slices, or
  2 small fresh onions, peeled and
  chopped
1 vegetable stock cube
900 ml/1½ pints boiling water
450 g/1 lb frozen Ratatouille Mix, or an
  equivalent weight of fresh vegetables
  including tomatoes, aubergines,
  courgettes, red and green peppers and
  onions, trimmed and diced
2 cloves garlic, crushed
freshly ground black pepper
1-2 tablespoons tomato purée
100 g/4 oz low fat Cheddar-type cheese,
  grated
2 tablespoons chopped fresh parsley

1 Place the barley in a 2.25 litre/4 pint bowl with the fennel seeds and onions. Crumble in the stock cube then pour in the boiling water and stir well.

2 Cover with cling film, pierce, and cook on HIGH for 45 minutes or until the barley is tender and the water has been absorbed.

3 Put the Ratatouille Mix or fresh vegetables into a 20 cm/8 inch deep round serving dish. If using fresh vegetables, add 4 tablespoons water. Cover with cling film, pierce, then cook on HIGH for 7 minutes. If using fresh vegetables, continue cooking and test at intervals of 1 minute until the vegetables have softened slightly.

4 Drain off the excess liquid and discard. Stir in the garlic, black pepper and tomato purée then cover again and cook for a further 7 minutes.

5 Stir two-thirds of the cheese and the parsley into the barley then spread the barley mixture over the vegetable layer.

6 To serve, sprinkle the remaining cheese over the top then brown under a preheated hot grill.

To freeze: when cool, overwrap with cling film, label and freeze. Use within 3 months. To serve, pierce the cling film then thaw on DEFROST for 15 minutes. Reheat on HIGH for 10 minutes or until heated through.

Fibre	● ● ●	Sugar	●
Fat	●	Salt	●

Carrot and celery bake

Serves 4
175 g/6 oz frozen baby carrots
4 sticks celery, cut into thin strips
4 spring onions, trimmed and halved
½ teaspoon fennel seeds
1 tablespoon lemon juice
1 tablespoon water
100 g/4 oz Mozzarella cheese
freshly ground black pepper

1 Place the baby carrots, celery and spring onions in a shallow dish. Sprinkle with the fennel seeds, lemon juice and water.

2 Cover with cling film, pierce, and cook on HIGH for 8 minutes, stirring halfway through the cooking time.

3 Drain off the liquid. Arrange slices of Mozzarella over the vegetables. Season well with black pepper.

4 Place under a preheated hot grill for a few minutes until the cheese is melted.

5 Serve immediately as an accompaniment to a main meal dish, such as Rosemary lamb (page 17) or Lemon chicken in mushroom sauce (page 12).

To freeze: not suitable for freezing.

Note: this recipe can be served as a vegetarian supper for 2 people.

Variations
Use fresh fennel, parsnips, courgettes or cauliflower instead of the frozen baby carrots.

Fibre	●	Sugar	●
Fat	●	Salt	● ● ●

Farmhouse beanfeast

Serves 4
225 g/8 oz frozen Farmhouse Style Mix, or an equivalent weight in fresh vegetables, including cauliflower and broccoli florets, sliced carrots and cut green beans
175 g/6 oz cooked chicken, diced
450 g/15.9 oz can baked beans
For the topping
50 g/2 oz fresh wholemeal breadcrumbs
50 g/2 oz Red Leicester cheese, grated
4 rashers frozen lean bacon, defrosted and rinded, to garnish

1 Place the vegetables in a straight-sided 1.5 litre/2½ pint dish. If using fresh vegetables add 4 tablespoons water. Cover with cling film, pierce, and cook on HIGH for 5 minutes. If using fresh vegetables, continue cooking and test at intervals of 1 minute until the vegetables have softened slightly.

2 Stir the chicken and beans into the vegetables. Cover again and cook on HIGH for 5 minutes, stirring the top layer carefully halfway through the cooking time.

3 Mix together the breadcrumbs and cheese. Sprinkle the mixture over the beans and brown under a preheated hot grill for a few minutes.

4 Stretch each rasher of bacon with the blunt edge of a knife. Cut each slice into 3 pieces. Roll up and arrange in a circle on kitchen paper and cook on HIGH for 2 minutes. Use to garnish the dish.

To freeze: not suitable for freezing.

Note: to serve as a vegetarian meal, omit the chicken and bacon rolls and put extra cheese on the top.

Variation
Try using a can of mixed beans or red kidney beans mixed with a small can of tomatoes, instead of the baked beans.

Fibre	● ● ●	Sugar	●
Fat	● ●	Salt	● ● ●

HEALTHY BREADS AND CAKES

Baking day has become an increasingly rare event in the kitchen calendar, as health considerations play an ever more important part in our lifestyle. But these recipes happily prove that with the right ingredients, homemade breads and cakes can provide healthy fibre, protein, vitamins and minerals and so justify their role as an important and enjoyable part of the family diet.

Wholemeal baps

Makes 16
750 g/1 ½ lb strong wholemeal flour
25 g/1 oz butter
8 g/0.2 oz sachet 'easy blend' dried yeast
½ teaspoon salt (optional)
450 ml/¾ pint water
1 teaspoon black treacle
a little milk, for brushing
toasted sesame seeds or flour, for dusting

1 Place the flour in a large bowl and warm for 1 minute on HIGH. Rub in the butter then stir in the yeast and the salt, if using.

2 Heat the water and treacle on HIGH for 30 seconds then stir it into the flour and yeast mixture to make a soft dough.

3 Knead for about 5 minutes on a lightly floured surface or in a mixer fitted with a dough hook for 1-2 minutes.

4 Divide the dough into 16 equal portions. Shape the portions into 'balls' then place in a circle around the edge of 2 large flat dinner plates dusted with flour. Flatten slightly with the palm of the hand to make bap shapes.

5 Place each plate inside a large plastic bag such as a clean bin liner and tie loosely at the top. Leave in a warm place for about 30 minutes until the baps have doubled in size.

6 Remove from the bags. Gently brush the surface of the baps with milk and dust with flour or sprinkle lightly with toasted sesame seeds. Cook 1 plate of baps at a time on HIGH for 3½-4½ minutes. Cool on a wire tray.

7 Serve the wholemeal baps filled with scrambled egg or low fat cheese, with salad for packed lunches or with Spicy burgers (page 66).

To freeze: pack into freezer bags. Seal and label. Use within 4 months. To defrost, place 4 baps at a time on to absorbent kitchen paper. Thaw on DEFROST for 1½ minutes.

Fibre ● ● ●	**Sugar** ●
Fat ●	**Salt** ● ●

Cheesy topped wholemeal scones

Makes 4 large or 8 small scones
175 g/6 oz wholemeal self-raising flour
50 g/2 oz white self-raising flour
1 teaspoon baking powder
1 teaspoon dry mustard
large pinch cayenne pepper
50 g/2 oz butter
100 g/4 oz mature Cheddar cheese, grated
1 egg, beaten
5-6 tablespoons milk, plus extra for brushing

1. Put all the dry ingredients into a large bowl. Rub in the butter, add half the cheese and all the egg and milk. Knead the mixture together to make a soft dough.

2. Roll out to an 18 cm/7 inch circle. Cut into 4 or 8 wedges. Space the pieces apart on greaseproof paper on a large plate. Cook on HIGH for 4½ minutes.

3. Brush with a little milk and sprinkle with the remaining cheese. Place the scones on a grill pan and place under the preheated hot grill of a conventional oven to brown. Cool on a wire rack.

To freeze: wrap in a double layer of cling film. Use within 3 months. To thaw, place scones on kitchen paper and cook on DEFROST for 3-4 minutes. Leave to stand for 5 minutes before serving.

Fibre	● ● ●	**Sugar**	●
Fat	● ●	**Salt**	● ● ●

Cheesy topped wholemeal scones: **Bottom** *Wholemeal baps*

Frosted coconut and carrot loaf

Serves 10
225 g/8 oz grated carrot
2 eggs, beaten
50 ml/2 fl oz vegetable oil
50 g/2 oz soft brown sugar
1 teaspoon vanilla essence
1 teaspoon ground cinnamon
1 teaspoon allspice
100 g/4 oz wholemeal self-raising flour
25 g/1 oz desiccated coconut
100 g/4 oz sultanas
50 ml/2 fl oz skimmed milk
For the frosting
150 g/5 oz low fat soft cheese
2-3 teaspoons thick honey
few drops vanilla essence
toasted coconut chips, to decorate

1 Combine all the cake ingredients and mix until very well blended.

2 Line a microwave cooking loaf mould measuring about 13×20 cm/5×8 inches with cling film. Spoon the mixture into the mould and smooth the surface.

3 Cook uncovered on HIGH for 10 minutes or until risen and just firm. Turn the loaf out of the mould and cool on a wire tray.

4 For the frosting, beat all the ingredients, except the coconut chips, together until smooth then chill for 1 hour. Spread the frosting evenly over the top of the cooled loaf. Then press the coconut down each side of the loaf to decorate. Store in the refrigerator.

To freeze: pack into a rigid container and label. Use within 3 months. To thaw an unfrosted loaf from frozen, unwrap the loaf and place between sheets of absorbent kitchen paper. Thaw on DEFROST for 4 minutes. If the loaf has been frozen with the frosting allow to thaw at room temperature for 4 hours.

| Fibre | ● ● ● | Sugar | ● ● ● |
| Fat | ● ● | Salt | ● ● |

Fig bars

Makes 12
For the filling
225 g/8 oz dried figs, chopped
100 g/4 oz frozen apple slices
2 tablespoons lemon juice
For the base and topping
75 g/3 oz butter
100 g/4 oz wholemeal self-raising flour
100 g/4 oz rolled oats
50 g/2 oz soft brown sugar
1 teaspoon ground cinnamon

1 Place all the filling ingredients in a small bowl. Cover with cling film, pierce, and cook on HIGH for 4 minutes. Spoon into a blender or food processor and process until smooth, or mash with a potato masher. Set aside to cool.

2 Rub the butter into the flour then stir in the oats and sugar.

3 Press three-quarters of the mixture into a 15 cm/6 inch square dish. Cook on MEDIUM for 6 minutes.

4 Spread the filling over the top. Add the cinnamon to the reserved flour and oat mixture and spoon over the filling. Return to the microwave cooker and cook on HIGH for 4 minutes. Leave in the dish to cool. When cold, cut into 12 bars.

To freeze: pack in a rigid container. Use within 3 months. To thaw, place the bars on a plate and cook on DEFROST for 2-3 minutes for 6 bars or 5 minutes for the whole batch. Leave to STAND for 5 minutes before serving.

Note: the fig bars are ideal for including in lunch boxes or serving as a dessert topped with a spoonful of hazelnut yogurt.

Variation
Use dates or dried apricots instead of figs and add a little orange rind and juice in place of the lemon.

| Fibre | ● ● ● | Sugar | ● ● |
| Fat | ● ● | Salt | ● ● |

Nutty shortbread

Makes 10 wedges
100 g/4 oz wholemeal self-raising flour
50 g/2 oz plain white flour
75 g/3 oz butter
50 g/2 oz brown sugar
40 g/1 ½ oz chopped mixed nuts, for the
topping

1   Measure the flour into a medium sized bowl. Rub in the butter until the mixture resembles fine breadcrumbs. Add the sugar then knead until it begins to stick together.

2   Press the mixture into an 18 cm/7 inch flan dish lined with cling film. Smooth the top with the back of a spoon and prick all over with a fork.

3   Sprinkle with the nuts. Cook on HIGH for 4½-5 minutes. Cut into 10 wedges. Leave in the dish to cool.

To freeze: When the shortbread has cooled, wrap each piece in foil or a double layer of cling film. Use within 3 months. To thaw, place the pieces on a plate and cook on DEFROST for about 1 ½ minutes for 2 pieces or 3 minutes for the whole batch. Leave to STAND for 2 to 3 minutes before serving.

Note: this shortbread makes a delicious base for cheesecakes, such as the Cherry cheesecake on page 48.

Fibre	● ● ●	Sugar	●
Fat	● ●	Salt	● ●

Muesli and sunflower seed triangles

Makes 10
65 g/2 ½ oz butter
3 tablespoons clear honey
150 g/ 5 oz unsweetened muesli with dried
fruit
2 tablespoons sunflower seeds
2 tablespoons wholemeal self-raising flour

1   Melt the butter and honey in a large bowl on HIGH for 1 ½-2 minutes.

2   Stir in the remaining ingredients until very well mixed then press into the base of a 20 cm/8 inch round shallow dish lined with cling film.

3   Cook, uncovered, on HIGH for 4 minutes or until risen and set. Allow to cool and harden before cutting into triangles.

To freeze: When cool wrap in foil. Label and use within 3 months. To serve, unwrap and place on absorbent kitchen paper. Thaw on DEFROST for 1 ½-2 minutes.

Fibre	● ● ●	Sugar	● ● ●
Fat	● ●	Salt	●

Ginger fingers

Makes 8
50 g/2 oz butter, softened
3 tablespoons black treacle
1-2 teaspoons ground ginger
1 teaspoon ground allspice
175 g/6 oz wholemeal self-raising flour
1 egg, beaten
120 ml/4 fl oz skimmed milk
1-2 tablespoons chopped stem ginger

1   Beat together the butter and treacle then sieve in the dry ingredients. Tip any bran left in the sieve into the bowl.

2   Beat in the egg and milk to make a soft consistency then stir in the ginger.

3   Line a microwave cooking loaf mould measuring 13×20 cm/5×8 inches with cling film. Spoon the mixture into the mould and smooth the surface. Cook on HIGH for 5 minutes or until evenly risen and just firm.

4   Carefully turn out of the mould and cool on a wire tray. When cold cut into bars.

To freeze: wrap in foil and label. Use within 3 months. To serve, unwrap and place between sheets of absorbent kitchen paper. Thaw on DEFROST for 2-3 minutes.

Fibre	● ● ●	Sugar	● ●
Fat	● ●	Salt	● ●

Tropical fruit cake

Serves 10
2 eggs
3 tablespoons black treacle
3 tablespoons vegetable oil
150 ml/¼ pint skimmed milk
100 g/4 oz ready-to-use prunes, stoned and
  chopped
100 g/4 oz ready-to-use apricots, chopped
350 g/12 oz mixed dried fruit
175 g/6 oz wholemeal self-raising flour
1 teaspoon baking powder
1½ teaspoons ground mixed spice
50 g/2 oz walnut halves

1 Beat together the eggs, black treacle, vegetable oil and skimmed milk in a large bowl.

2 Stir in the dried fruits then sieve in the flour, baking powder and spice. Tip any bran left in the sieve into the bowl, then mix together thoroughly.

3 Reserve six walnut halves then chop the remainder and fold into the cake mixture. Pour into a 18 cm/7 inch soufflé dish or suitable round microwave cooking mould that has been lined with greaseproof paper.

4 Smooth the surface then place the reserved walnuts around the edge. Bake on DEFROST for 28 minutes or until evenly risen and just firm to the touch. The surface may look moist, but will dry as it cools.

5 Remove from the container and remove the lining paper before cooling.

To freeze: wrap in foil and label. Use within 3 months. To serve, unwrap the cake and place between sheets of absorbent kitchen paper. Thaw on DEFROST for 5 minutes and leave to STAND to complete thawing.

| Fibre | ● ● ● | Sugar | ● ● |
| Fat | ● ● | Salt | ● ● |

Honey and banana cake

Serves 8
40 g/1½ oz butter
4 tablespoons honey
1 teaspoon ground cinnamon
150 ml/¼ pint skimmed milk
200 g/7 oz wholemeal flour
2 teaspoons baking powder
2 egg whites
For the topping
2 tablespoons honey
25 g/1 oz butter
1 banana, peeled
25 g/1 oz flaked almonds, toasted

1 Place the butter, honey and cinnamon in a large bowl. Cook on HIGH for 30 seconds. Stir in the milk. Add the flour and baking powder.

2 Whisk the egg whites until stiff. Stir about 1 tablespoon into the mixture, then stir in the remainder quickly.

3 Place a circle of greased greaseproof paper in the base of a 1.5 litre/2½ pint soufflé dish, then pour in the cake mixture. Cook on HIGH for 5 minutes. Leave to STAND for 10 minutes, then turn out on to a wire rack to cool.

4 Put the honey and butter in a small bowl. Cook on HIGH for 1 minute. Whisk until the mixture starts to cool and thicken. Spoon about a third over the cake.

5 Slice the banana, then arrange overlapping slices round the top edge of the cake. Fill the centre with the almonds. Spoon the remaining glaze over the banana and almonds. Leave for 10 minutes to set. Transfer to a serving plate. Eat on the day it is made.

To freeze: not suitable for freezing.

| Fibre | ● ● ● | Sugar | ● ● |
| Fat | ● ● | Salt | ● ● |

From top left, clockwise *Honey and banana cake; Frosted coconut and carrot loaf (page 44); Muesli and sunflower seed triangles (page 45); Ginger fingers (page 45); Fig bars (page 44)*

HEALTHY PUDDINGS AND DESSERTS

Healthy eating doesn't mean that we should forgo
the part of the meal that many of us enjoy most!
The variety of frozen fruits offered by a well-stocked freezer can quickly be
transformed by clever use of
the microwave cooker, to make delicious and nutritious desserts.
The old saying 'a little of what you fancy does you good' is especially true when any
of the recipes from this chapter are on the menu. You'll never believe that healthy
eating could taste – or look – so good!

Cherry cheesecake

Serves 6

½ quantity Nutty shortbread dough (page
45), excluding nuts
225 g/8 oz frozen black cherries

For the topping

225 g/8 oz low fat soft cheese
25 g/1 oz soft brown sugar
½ teaspoon ground cinnamon
1 egg
1 tablespoon natural yogurt

1 Press the shortbread dough into an
18 cm/7 inch flan dish. Smooth the top
and prick the mixture all over with a fork.
Cook on HIGH for 2 minutes.

2 Place the cherries in a bowl. Thaw on
DEFROST for 4 minutes. Strain off the
juice, reserve if liked (see below). Spoon the
cherries over the shortbread base.

3 Place the soft cheese, sugar, cinnamon
and egg in a medium bowl and mix until
smooth. Cook on MEDIUM for 3 minutes,
whisking halfway through the cooking time.
Whisk well until the mixture is smooth. Stir in
the yogurt.

4 Spoon the cheese topping over the
cherries and make decorative swirls, if
you wish, on the topping using the glaze
mentioned in the **Notes** below. Chill and set.

To freeze: The finished cheesecake is not
suitable for freezing, however the shortbread
base can be frozen. Cool the shortbread
base, then wrap in a double layer of cling film.
Use within 3 months. To thaw, place the
shortbread on a piece of absorbent kitchen
paper and cook on DEFROST for 3 minutes.
Leave to STAND for 2-3 minutes before
using.

Notes: to remove the cheesecake from the
dish for serving, line the dish with cling film
before putting in the shortbread base.
This cheesecake is best eaten on the day it is
made.
Thicken the reserved cherry juice with
arrowroot to make a glaze if liked. Use 1
teaspoon arrowroot and blend with the
cherry juice. Cook on HIGH for 1-2 minutes,
or until the glaze is clear and thickened.

Variations

Almost any type of fruit can be used instead
of the cherries. For a blackberry cheesecake:
use 225 g/8 oz frozen blackberries and add
1 teaspoon of ground mixed spice to the
topping mixture. For a gooseberry
cheesecake: use 225 g/8 oz frozen
gooseberries and add ½ teaspoon ground
ginger, or 1 tablespoon finely chopped stem
ginger to the topping mixture.

| Fibre | ● | Sugar | ● ● |
| Fat | ● ● | Salt | ● |

Gooseberry and strawberry meringue

Serves 4
350 g/12 oz frozen gooseberries
3 tablespoons clear honey
225 g/8 oz frozen strawberries
2 egg whites
50 g/2 oz soft brown sugar
2 tablespoons chopped mixed
  nuts, toasted

1 Place the frozen gooseberries in a heatproof glass serving bowl with the honey. Cover with cling film, pierce, and cook on HIGH for 6 minutes or until soft, stirring once during the cooking time.

2 Mash the gooseberries slightly then stir in the frozen strawberries. Return to the microwave cooker and cook for a further 1 minute.

3 Whisk the egg whites until frothy. Add half the sugar then whisk again. Beat in the remaining sugar and whisk again until very stiff and glossy.

4 Spoon or pipe the meringue over the fruit. Sprinkle with the nuts then cook on HIGH for 2 minutes. Serve immediately.

To freeze: not suitable for freezing.

Variations
This dessert is delicious made with almost any combination of frozen or fresh fruits. For a Blackberry and apple meringue: use 275 g/10 oz frozen blackberries and 275 g/10 oz frozen apple slices. For a Rhubarb and orange meringue: use 350 g/12 oz frozen rhubarb and 1 × 170 g/6 oz can mandarin segments, drained. For a Banana and raspberry meringue (a children's favourite): use 3 small bananas, peeled and sliced and 225 g/8 oz frozen raspberries.
As a change from nuts, sprinkle the meringue with toasted coconut chips or toasted desiccated coconut.

Fibre	● ●	Sugar	● ● ●
Fat	●	Salt	●

Rhubarb and blackcurrant summer puddings

Serves 4
275 g/10 oz frozen rhubarb
275 g/10 oz frozen blackcurrants
2 tablespoons clear honey
2 teaspoons stem ginger, finely chopped
2 tablespoons stem ginger syrup
8-9 slices wholemeal bread
To serve
Greek strained natural yogurt
4 sprigs of fresh mint (optional)

1 Put the frozen rhubarb and blackcurrants into a bowl with the honey, stem ginger and syrup. Cover with cling film, pierce, and cook on HIGH for 9-10 minutes or until the fruit is tender and juicy.

2 Remove the crusts from the bread then flatten the slices with a rolling pin.

3 Cut 4 slices of the bread into strips then line 4 × 150 ml/¼ pint teacups with the strips. Stamp out tops with another cup then use the trimmings to fill in any gaps.

4 Spoon the fruit into the bread-lined cups and press the rounds firmly on top to enclose the filling completely. Spoon over any juice then cover with cling film and chill thoroughly, preferably overnight.

5 To serve, run a knife round the inside of each cup then turn on to individual serving plates. Serve topped with Greek strained yogurt and decorate with the sprigs of mint, if liked.

To freeze: keep covered and label. Use within 3 months. To serve, thaw for 4 hours at room temperature.

Notes: if preferred, replace the ginger syrup with extra honey.
  This dessert can also be made with a mixture of raspberries, blackberries and redcurrants.

Fibre	● ● ●	Sugar	● ●
Fat	● ●	Salt	●

Above *Brightly glazed apples*

Brightly glazed apples

Serves 4
4 green-skinned dessert apples, about
 150 g/5 oz each, cored
100 g/4 oz frozen blackberries
100 g/4 oz frozen blackcurrants
2 tablespoons demerara sugar
1 tablespoon chopped fresh mint (optional)
2 teaspoons arrowroot
2 tablespoons water
4 small sprigs fresh mint, to decorate
 (optional)

1 Score round the centre of each apple with a sharp knife to prevent the skins splitting. Arrange them in a circle around the edge of a shallow dish.

2 Mix the blackberries, blackcurrants, sugar and mint (if using) together. Spoon half the mixture into the apples pressing it down well and spoon the remainder around the apples on the dish.

3 Cover the apples loosely with cling film, pierce, and cook on HIGH for 8 minutes.

4 Spoon all the blackberries and blackcurrants from the dish into the apples. Using a draining spoon, transfer the apples to a serving plate.

5 Blend the arrowroot and water together in a small jug, then add all the fruit cooking liquid.

6 Mix well and cook on HIGH for 2 minutes, stirring halfway through the cooking time. The glaze should be smooth and of a pouring consistency.

7 Pour the glaze over the apples to coat them completely. Decorate with the mint sprigs if liked and serve the apples warm or cold.

To freeze: not suitable for freezing.

Note: these apples can be cooked in advance and reheated in the microwave on HIGH for 1 minute for 1 apple or 3 minutes for 4 apples.

Variation
Use any combination of fruits you wish for stuffing the apples, though a red fruit element will always make the dish look its best. Gooseberries and cherries, with a little mixed spice, make a good combination, as do redcurrants and chopped orange.

Fibre		Sugar	
Fat	● ● ●	Salt	● ●

Right *Cherry cheesecake (page 48)*
Raspberry and orange sorbet (page 52)

Raspberry and orange sorbet

Serves 4
225 g/8 oz frozen raspberries
2 egg whites
2-3 tablespoons clear honey
½ teaspoon grated orange rind
150 ml/¼ pint thick set or Greek strained
    natural yogurt
To serve
fresh orange segments
raspberries, defrosted
fresh mint sprigs (optional)

1 Put the frozen raspberries in a bowl, cover with cling film and pierce. Cook on HIGH for 2 minutes or until thawed and slightly softened.

2 Whisk the egg whites until stiff. Add the honey and whisk again until glossy.

3 Fold the raspberry mixture, orange rind and yogurt into the egg whites, then pour into a rigid container and cover.

4 Place in the freezer and freeze for about 3-4 hours or until firm.

5 To serve, place scoops of the sorbet on plates with segments of fresh orange and a few raspberries. Decorate with sprigs of mint if liked.

To freeze: cover with a double layer of cling film and use within 1 month.

Note: if the sorbet is too hard to serve straight from the freezer soften slightly in the microwave cooker on DEFROST for 1-2 minutes.

Variations
Sorbet always makes a healthy dessert to offer family or friends for special occasions. Try Strawberry sorbet: use 225 g/8 oz frozen strawberries and ½ teaspoon grated lemon rind. For a Rhubarb and almond sorbet, use 225 g/8 oz frozen rhubarb and 25 g/1 oz flaked almonds.

| Fibre | • • | Sugar | • • |
| Fat | • • | Salt | • |

Fruity sponge puddings with marmalade sauce

Serves 4
3 tablespoons thick cut marmalade
40 g/1 ½ oz butter, softened
50 g/2 oz wholemeal self-raising flour
½ teaspoon baking powder
2 large pinches of ground cloves
1 egg, beaten
50 g/2 oz mixed dried fruit
1-2 tablespoons skimmed milk

1 Beat 2 tablespoons of the marmalade into the butter then sieve in the flour, baking powder and ground cloves.

2 Stir in the egg, fruit and enough skimmed milk to give a soft consistency, then divide between 4 lightly greased teacups (see **Note**).

3 Cook, uncovered, on HIGH for 2½ minutes then STAND for 1 minute before turning out.

4 Heat the remaining marmalade on HIGH for 30 seconds to 1 minute or until melted. Spoon a little marmalade over each sponge pudding before serving.

To freeze: not suitable for freezing.

Note: make sure that the teacups in which the puddings are cooked do not have metallic decorations, as these may cause a malfunction in the microwave cooker.

| Fibre | • • | Sugar | • • |
| Fat | • • | Salt | • • |

Red fruit and ginger fool

Serves 6
225 g/8 oz frozen rhubarb
225 g/8 oz frozen raspberries
25 g/1 oz stem ginger, finely chopped
15 g/½ oz powdered gelatine
3 tablespoons water
3 tablespoons honey
300 ml/½ pint rhubarb or raspberry yogurt
25 g/1 oz stem ginger, to decorate

1 Place the fruit and stem ginger in a bowl. Cover with cling film, pierce, and cook on HIGH for 5 minutes, stirring once during the cooking time. Leave to STAND for 5 minutes.

2 Pour the fruit and ginger mixture into a blender or food processor and process until smooth.

3 Sprinkle the gelatine into the water in a cup. Cook on DEFROST for 1 minute or until dissolved. Whisk into the purée with the honey. Cool for 15 minutes.

4 Whisk the yogurt into the purée. Pour the mixture into individual glasses or dishes and leave until set.

5 Decorate each glass with a little of the chopped ginger.

To freeze: not suitable for freezing.

Note: this dish can be made one day in advance. Keep chilled.

Variation
Try varying the fruits and fruit yogurts.

| Fibre | ● | Sugar | ● ● |
| Fat | ● | Salt | ● |

Fruit medley with crunchy coriander topping

Serves 4-6
750 g/1½ lb frozen apple slices
50 g/2 oz ready-to-eat dried apricots, roughly chopped
1 tablespoon demerara sugar
1 banana, sliced and tossed in a little lemon juice
For the topping
25 g/1 oz butter
75 g/3 oz wheatflakes
25 g/1 oz raisins
25 g/1 oz rolled oats
1 tablespoon demerara sugar
2 teaspoons coriander seeds, coarsely crushed
natural yogurt, to serve

1 Place the apples, chopped apricots and sugar in a 1.5 litre/2½ pint dish. Cover with cling film, pierce, and cook on HIGH for 6 minutes, stirring halfway through the cooking time. Add the banana slices.

2 To make the topping, place the butter in a medium sized bowl. Cook on HIGH for 30 seconds. Stir in the wheatflakes, raisins, oats and sugar.

3 Spoon the topping mixture over the fruit. Sprinkle with the coriander seeds and cook on HIGH for 2 minutes. Serve with natural yogurt.

To freeze: not suitable for freezing.

Variation
Replace the banana with a few chopped dates or figs, and vary the cereals.

| Fibre | ● ● ● | Sugar | ● |
| Fat | ● | Salt | ● |

Tropical fruit salad

Serves 4
1 orange, peeled and segmented
1 paw paw, peeled, deseeded and sliced
¼ melon, skin removed, deseeded and diced
1 kiwi fruit, peeled and sliced
1 banana, peeled and sliced
1 tablespoon lemon juice
2 tablespoons Malibu (optional)
150 ml/¼ pint frozen orange juice, defrosted
50 g/2 oz flaked almonds

1 Place the fruit in a large glass bowl, then stir in the lemon juice, Malibu, if using, and orange juice. Leave for 1 hour.

2 Meanwhile, spread the almonds on a sheet of greaseproof paper, place in the microwave cooker and cook on HIGH for 2-3 minutes or until brown. Sprinkle the salad with almonds before serving.

| Fibre | ● ● ● | Sugar | ● ● |
| Fat | | Salt | |

Summer peaches

Serves 4
4 ripe fresh peaches, halved, stoned and
brushed with lemon juice
For the topping
8 tablespoons thick set natural yogurt
2 tablespoons honey
75 g/3 oz frozen raspberries
To decorate
peach or lemon verbena leaves
demerara sugar

1 Prick the skins of the peaches. Arrange cut side up in a circle around a shallow dish. Cover with cling film, pierce, and cook on DEFROST for 7 minutes. Keep covered

and leave to cool.

2 Blend the yogurt and honey. Mash a third of the raspberries with a fork and add to the yogurt mixture. Spoon into the peach hollows. Decorate with the remaining raspberries, leaves and demerara sugar.

To freeze: not suitable for freezing.

Variation
Omit the honey and just sprinkle demerara sugar on top of the yogurt mixture before decorating with the fruit.

Fibre	• •	Sugar	• •
Fat	•	Salt	•

Summer peaches

Top *Kissel; Nutty shortbread (page 45)*

Kissel

Serves 4-6

*6 tablespoons grenadine or blackcurrant
  fruit syrup
175 g/6 oz frozen cherries
175 g/6 oz frozen blackcurrants
175 g/6 oz frozen blackberries
175 g/6 oz frozen raspberries
150 ml/¼ pint natural yogurt, to serve*

1 Measure the fruit syrup into a large
   bowl. Add the cherries, blackcurrants
and blackberries. Cover with cling film and
pierce.

2 Thaw on DEFROST for 5 minutes. Stir,
   cover again and cook on DEFROST for
a further 4-5 minutes.

3 Stir in the raspberries. Leave to STAND,
   covered for about 30 minutes or until
the raspberries have thawed.

4 Serve with natural yogurt and Nutty
   shortbread (page 45).

To freeze: not suitable for freezing.

| Fibre | ● ● ● | Sugar | ● ● |
| Fat | ● | Salt | ● |

HEALTHY BREAKFASTS AND LUNCH BOXES

Eating healthy meals at home will be to no avail if the family are eating the wrong types of food at other times.
Try a selection of recipes from this chapter to add to your breakfast and packed lunch repertoire: wholesome ingredients presented attractively will mean less temptation to eat junk food snacks and sweets between meals.

Morning compote with grapefruit

Serves 4-6
225 g/8 oz mixed dried fruit salad, including prunes, apricots, peaches, pears and apples
450 ml/¾ pint hot weak Earl Grey tea
1 large grapefruit
To serve
natural yogurt
muesli

1 Put the dried fruit into a heatproof serving bowl and pour over the hot tea. Cover with cling film, pierce, and cook on HIGH for 5 minutes. Leave to cool. The fruit will plump up as it cools.

2 Cut the peel and pith away from the grapefruit with a sharp knife. Cut the fruit into segments by slicing the knife between the membranes, taking care to collect any juices. Place the segments in the serving dish with the dried fruit mixture and any juice collected while the grapefruit was being segmented.

3 Halve or quarter any fruits that are large. Serve chilled topped with yogurt and sprinkled with muesli.

To freeze: pack into a rigid container and label. Use within 3 months. To serve, thaw on DEFROST for about 10 minutes.

Note: as an alternative use 100 g/4 oz each dried apricots and figs instead of the mixed dried fruit salad.

Fibre ● ● ●	Sugar ●
Fat ●	Salt ●

Sultana porridge

Serves 2
4 rounded tablespoons rolled oats
2 teaspoons medium oatmeal
300 ml/½ pint skimmed milk
2 tablespoons sultanas
skimmed milk, to serve (optional)

1 Divide the oats, oatmeal and skimmed milk between 2 cereal bowls and stir well. Cook on HIGH for 3 minutes, stirring the porridge mixture once during cooking.

2 Add the sultanas. Cook on HIGH for a further ½-1 minute. Serve the porridge with extra skimmed milk, if liked.

To freeze: not suitable for freezing.

Variations
Sprinkle with demerara sugar or ground cinnamon or 2 teaspoons chopped hazelnuts, toasted.

Fibre ● ● ●	Sugar ●
Fat ●	Salt ●

Eggs on waffles

Serves 4
4 frozen potato waffles
about 300 ml/½ pint boiling water, mixed
  with 1 teaspoon vinegar
4 eggs
freshly ground black pepper

1 Arrange the waffles on a flat plate and cook on HIGH for 2 minutes.

2 Transfer the waffles to a grill pan and place under the preheated hot grill of a conventional oven: brown on both sides while cooking the eggs.

3 Half fill 4 teacups with the water and vinegar: quickly crack an egg into each cup. Pierce the yolks with a cocktail stick.

4 Cook on MEDIUM for 4 minutes. Leave to STAND for 1 minute. Drain and serve an egg on each waffle. Season with pepper.

To freeze: not suitable for freezing.

Note: it is important to cook the eggs quickly, once broken into the cups.

Variation
For a substantial breakfast or light supper, place a slice of ham on top of each waffle and spread on a little mustard. Serve the egg on top of the ham.

Fibre	●	Sugar	●
Fat	● ●	Salt	● ●

Sesame chicken

Serves 4-8
8 frozen chicken drumsticks, thawed,
  skinned and trimmed of fat
1 tablespoon honey
1 tablespoon soy sauce
1-2 teaspoons ground ginger
For the coating
100 g/4 oz wholemeal breadcrumbs
3 tablespoons sesame seeds
2 tablespoons chopped fresh parsley
freshly ground black pepper

1 Arrange the drumsticks in a shallow dish radiating from the centre, with the knuckle ends in the centre. Mix the honey, soy sauce and ginger and brush over the drumsticks.

2 Cover with cling film, pierce, and cook on HIGH for 4 minutes. Drain off the juices and reserve. Turn the drumsticks over, cover again and return to the microwave cooker and cook a further 4-5 minutes or until the meat juices run clear when the flesh is pierced with a knife.

3 To make the coating, mix the breadcrumbs and sesame seeds on a piece of foil. Place on a grill pan and brown under a preheated hot grill, stirring occasionally, until crispy and lightly browned. Remove from the heat and add the parsley and seasoning.

4 Brush each drumstick with the cooking juices then dip in the sesame seed mixture, turning until completely coated. Place on a plate to cool.

5 Wrap in foil for carrying in a lunch or picnic box.

To freeze: pack into a rigid container and label. Use within 2 months. To serve, thaw 4 chicken drumsticks at a time, for 5 minutes on DEFROST. Reheat on HIGH for 3 minutes. Repeat with the remaining 4 chicken pieces.

Note: chicken drumsticks are easily transported for picnics and are convenient to eat with the fingers. Try Tandoori-style chicken (page 12) as an alternative.

Variations
For Sesame and poppy seed chicken: use 2 tablespoons of sesame seeds and 1 tablespoon poppy seeds. The poppy seeds have a slightly stronger taste than the sesame seeds. For a Middle-eastern flavour use 2 tablespoons chopped fresh coriander instead of the parsley.

Fibre	● ●	Sugar	● ●
Fat	●	Salt	● ●

Salade niçoise

Serves 2

175 g/6oz frozen whole French beans
4 tablespoons boiling water
½ small iceberg lettuce, cut into wedges
1-2 tomatoes, cut into wedges
1 small onion, peeled and sliced into rings
198 g/7 oz can tuna in brine, drained
2 teaspoons capers

For the dressing

1 tablespoon vinegar
1 tablespoon olive oil
1 clove garlic, crushed
freshly ground black pepper
1 tablespoon chopped fresh chives or
*   parsley*
2 hard-boiled eggs, to garnish

1 Place the beans in a bowl with the water. Cover with cling film, pierce, then cook on HIGH for 5 minutes. Drain and cool.

2 Place the lettuce wedges in a rigid plastic container with the beans, tomatoes, onion, tuna and capers. Cut each egg into 4 wedges then arrange on top. Alternatively divide between individual containers.

3 Mix the dressing ingredients in a screwtop jar, shaking well to combine. Pour over the salad or store the dressing separately and toss together just before serving.

To freeze: not suitable for freezing.

Note: this type of salad is perfect for picnics and special packed lunches. It can be made the night before and stored in the refrigerator. Serves 4 as part of a picnic.

Fibre	●	Sugar	●
Fat	● ●	Salt	● ●

Piquant potato and bean salad

Serves 1

100 g/4 oz new potatoes, scrubbed and
*   diced*
3 tablespoons water
1 tablespoon white wine vinegar or cider
*   vinegar*
1 clove garlic, crushed
¼ teaspoon English mustard powder
freshly ground black pepper
100 g/4 oz frozen broad beans
50 g/2 oz lean smoked ham, cut into strips
1 tablespoon chopped fresh parsley
1 tablespoon chopped fresh chives or spring
*   onion tops*

1 Put the potatoes into a bowl with the
  water, vinegar, garlic and mustard.

Season with plenty of black pepper then
cover with cling film and pierce.

2 Cook on HIGH for 5 minutes. Stir in the
  beans, then cover again and cook for a
further 4 minutes. STAND for 5 minutes.

3 Toss the smoked ham and herbs with
  the potato mixture and serve.

To freeze: overwrap with cling film and label.
Use within 1 month. To serve, pierce the cling
film and thaw on DEFROST for 2-3 minutes.

Note: strips of raw red and green pepper can
be stirred in for added colour.

| Fibre | ● ● ● | Sugar | ● |
| Fat | ● | Salt | ● ● ● |

Left *Piquant potato and bean salad;* **Centre** *Salade niçoise;* **Right** *Sesame chicken (page 57)*

Breakfast baps

Serves 2
2 eggs
1 tablespoon dried skimmed milk powder
freshly ground black pepper
knob of butter
3 tablespoons frozen sweetcorn
2 wholemeal baps (page 42)
1 tomato, sliced

1 Whisk the eggs and milk powder. Season well with pepper and add the butter. Cook on MEDIUM for 2 minutes, stirring halfway through the cooking time.

2 Add the sweetcorn and cook on MEDIUM a further 2 minutes.

3 Split the baps. Arrange the tomato slices on the 2 bases. To warm the bases and tops cook on MEDIUM for 30 seconds. Divide the scrambled egg mixture between the 2 baps and serve immediately.

To freeze: not suitable for freezing.

Note: the scrambled egg mixture could be left to cool and then spread into baps for a packed lunch.

Fibre	● ● ●	Sugar	●
Fat	● ●	Salt	●

Lemony kipper pâté

Serves 1 (fills 2 baps)
100 g/4 oz frozen kipper fillets, defrosted
25 g/1 oz frozen onion slices, or ¼ small
    fresh onion, chopped
1-1½ tablespoons chopped parsley
freshly ground black pepper
2 teaspoons lemon juice
½ teaspoon grated lemon rind (optional)
chopped parsley, to garnish

1 Place the kipper and onion on a dish. Cover with cling film, pierce, and cook on HIGH for 2 minutes.

2 Allow to STAND for 5 minutes then skin the fish and remove any bones.

3 Place the fish in a food processor or blender together with the onion, parsley, black pepper, lemon juice and lemon rind if using. Process to a purée then spoon into a ramekin dish and sprinkle with the parsley, to garnish.

4 Serve in Wholemeal baps (page 42) with crisp shredded lettuce and slices of fresh tomato.

To freeze: not suitable for freezing.

Note: for a firmer textured pâté beat 25 g/ 1 oz low fat soft cheese into the mixture.

Fibre	●	Sugar	●
Fat	● ●	Salt	● ● ●

Winter vegetable soup

Serves 4, makes approximately 450 ml/1 pint
225 g/8 oz potatoes, peeled and diced
100 g/4 oz frozen onion slices, or 1 small
    fresh onion, peeled and sliced
knob of butter
350 g/12 oz frozen Stewpack vegetables, or
    an equivalent weight of fresh vegetables
    including, carrots, swedes, turnips,
    onions and celery, peeled and diced
½ teaspoon ground nutmeg
freshly ground black pepper
300 ml/½ pint hot vegetable stock
To finish
150 ml/¼ pint skimmed milk, or water
100 g/4 oz frozen sliced cabbage

1 Place the potatoes, onion and butter in a large bowl. Cover with cling film, pierce, and cook on HIGH for 5 minutes.

2 Stir in the Stewpack or fresh vegetables, spice and seasoning. Cover again and return to the microwave cooker and cook on HIGH for 5 minutes.

3 Add the hot stock, cover again and cook on HIGH for a further 2 minutes. If fresh vegetables have been used they may take slightly longer to cook, so allow extra cooking time.

4 Cool for a few minutes then pour into a blender or food processor and process until smooth.

5 Return the soup to the bowl, stir in the milk or water and cabbage and cook on HIGH for 3 minutes or until the soup is heated through.

6 Sprinkle with freshly ground black pepper and serve with hot crusty wholemeal rolls.

To freeze: after step 4 has been completed, allow to cool fully then pour into a rigid container, leaving 2.5 cm/1 inch headspace. Use within 3 months. To thaw, remove lid, and cook on DEFROST for 5 minutes. Turn into a large bowl and cook on HIGH for 8-10 minutes, stirring occasionally until the soup is hot. Proceed to step 5.

Note: this soup can be made to the end of step 4 and cooled for use later in the day or kept hot in a vacuum flask for a packed lunch or picnic.

Variations

Use any combination of frozen vegetables instead of the Stewpack. Try using a mixture of frozen peas and broad beans, together with a little fresh or dried mint. Frozen cauliflower and courgettes make another good combination: add a little fresh or dried thyme.

Fibre	● ●		**Sugar**	●
Fat	●		**Salt**	●

St Clement's carrot soup

Serves 4-6

100 g/4 oz frozen onion slices or 1 small
*   fresh onion, peeled and sliced*
450 g/1 lb frozen carrots (whole or sliced)
15 g/½ oz butter
3 tablespoons orange juice
3 tablespoons sherry
600 ml/1 pint hot vegetable or chicken stock
freshly ground black pepper
150 ml/¼ pint skimmed milk
snipped chives, to garnish

1 Place the onion, carrots and butter in a large bowl. Cover with cling film, pierce, and cook on HIGH for 10 minutes. Stir once during cooking.

2 Add the orange juice, sherry, half the stock and season to taste with pepper. Cover again, pierce, and cook on HIGH for 10 minutes, stirring once during cooking.

3 Pour the cooked vegetables into a liquidizer or food processor and blend until smooth. Return the purée to the bowl and stir in the remaining stock.

4 Add the milk and cook on HIGH for about 4 minutes, or until piping hot. Adjust seasoning if necessary.

5 If serving as part of a picnic, pour immediately into a vacuum flask and seal tightly. Serve sprinkled with snipped chives, packed separately.

To freeze: after step 3 has been completed, pour the soup into a rigid container, leaving 2.5 cm/1 inch headspace. Use within 3 months. To thaw and reheat, remove the lid of the container. Thaw on DEFROST for 5 minutes. Turn into a large bowl, breaking up the block. Cover with cling film, pierce, and cook on HIGH for 15 minutes stirring twice during cooking. Add the milk and continue with step 4.

Note: for an extra filling lunchtime soup, serve St Clement's carrot soup with Herbed wholemeal croûtons. To serve with soup for 4-6, cut 3 thick slices of wholemeal or granary bread into 2.5 cm/1 inch cubes. Pour 2 tablespoons grapeseed or sunflower seed oil into a medium sized bowl and cook on HIGH for 1 minute. Stir in the cubes of bread and 1 tablespoon chopped fresh mixed herbs, or 1 teaspoon dried mixed herbs. Cook on HIGH for 2 minutes. Transfer the croûtons to a large plate, covered with a piece of absorbent kitchen paper, and leave to STAND for 2-3 minutes or until the croûtons are crisp.

Fibre	● ●		**Sugar**	●
Fat	●		**Salt**	●

HEALTHY FAST FOOD

Fast food is usually considered unhealthy in the extreme,
but the recipes that follow in this chapter prove otherwise.
Keeping a well-stocked freezer means that the very healthiest of foods
will always be to hand, and with the microwave cooker,
healthy cooking rapidly becomes fast food.

Herby corn cobs

Serves 2
2 frozen corn on the cob
2 tablespoons chopped fresh mixed herbs
    or 2 teaspoons dried mixed herbs
2 cloves garlic, crushed
2 tablespoons lemon juice
freshly ground black pepper

1 Place the corn on the cob in a shallow
dish. Mix half the herbs with the other
ingredients and sprinkle over the corn.

2 Cover with cling film, pierce, and cook
on HIGH for 5 minutes. Turn the corn
over, cover again and cook on HIGH for a
further 4 minutes.

3 Sprinkle over the remaining herbs and
serve immediately as a starter or
snack.

To freeze: not suitable for freezing.

| Fibre | ● ● ● | Sugar |
| Fat | | Salt |

Herby corn cobs

Devilled chicken livers

Devilled chicken livers

Serves 2-3

225 g/8 oz frozen chicken livers, defrosted
1 tablespoon sherry
1 tablespoon Worcestershire sauce
few drops Tabasco sauce
1 tablespoon tomato purée
1 teaspoon mustard powder
1 teaspoon dried rosemary
freshly ground black pepper
175 g/6 oz frozen sliced mushrooms,
*   defrosted and drained*
50 g/2 oz green and black grapes, halved
*   and deseeded*
4-6 slices granary bread, toasted

1   Cut the chicken livers into 2.5 cm/1 inch
    pieces. Mix the sherry, Worcestershire
sauce and Tabasco sauce, tomato purée,
mustard, rosemary and seasoning in a
medium sized bowl. Stir in the chicken livers.
Cover with cling film, pierce, and cook on
MEDIUM for 2 minutes.

2   Add the mushrooms and stir. Cover
    again and cook on MEDIUM for a further
2 minutes.

3   Stir the grapes into the mixture. Cover
    and STAND for 1 minute. Spoon on to
the toast and serve immediately.

To freeze: not suitable for freezing.

Note: the Devilled chicken livers are
delicious tossed with freshly cooked pasta.

Fibre	● ●	Sugar	●
Fat	●	Salt	● ●

Pasta twists with herby cheese and walnut sauce

Serves 1
50 g/2 oz small green pasta twists
600 ml/1 pint boiling water
For the cheese and walnut sauce
2-3 tablespoons low fat soft cheese with
*   garlic and herbs*
1 clove garlic, crushed
1 tablespoon chopped fresh parsley
1 tablespoon chopped fresh basil
*   or 2 teaspoons dried basil*
1½ tablespoons walnut pieces, chopped
1-2 tablespoons skimmed milk
freshly ground black pepper

1   Put the pasta in a 1.75 litre/3 pint bowl.
    Pour over the water, cover with cling
film, pierce, and cook on HIGH for 4-5
minutes. The pasta should be 'al dente' or
just firm to the bite.

2   Meanwhile mix together all the sauce
    ingredients and season with pepper.

3   Drain the pasta and place in a serving
    dish. Add the prepared cheese and
walnut sauce, toss and serve immediately.

To freeze: not suitable for freezing.

Note: to serve 2 portions, cook 100 g/4 oz
pasta in the boiling water for 5-6 minutes.
Double the sauce ingredients and serve as
above.

| Fibre | ● ● | Sugar | ● |
| Fat | ● ● | Salt | ● |

Seafood waffles

Serves 2
4 frozen potato waffles
2 tomatoes sliced
100 g/4 oz cottage cheese
100 g-175 g/4 oz-6 oz frozen crab meat,
*   defrosted*
4 spring onions, trimmed, chopped
few drops Tabasco sauce
freshly ground black pepper
lime wedges, to serve

1   Arrange the waffles on a large plate.
    Cook on HIGH for 2 minutes. Transfer to
a grill pan and place under a preheated hot
grill.

2   Grill one side until crisp and brown. Turn
    the waffles over and grill the other side
for 1 minute. Arrange the tomato slices on
top and grill for a few more minutes.

3   Mix the cheese, crab meat, spring
    onions and Tabasco. Divide the mixture
between the waffles and season well. Serve
immediately with lime wedges.

To freeze: not suitable for freezing.

| Fibre | ● | Sugar | ● |
| Fat | ● | Salt | ● ● |

Mexican omelette

Serves 2
8 tablespoons frozen Mexican Mix or an
*   equivalent weight of fresh vegetables*
*   including diced red and green peppers,*
*   sweetcorn and chopped onion*
50 g/2 oz lean ham, chopped
3 eggs, separated
3 tablespoons skimmed milk
freshly ground black pepper
2 teaspoons chopped fresh marjoram or
*   1 teaspoon dried oregano*
15 g/½ oz butter
a little paprika

1   Place the vegetables in a medium sized
    bowl. If using fresh vegetables, use 2
tablespoons water. Cover with cling film,
pierce, and cook on HIGH for 5 minutes then
drain if necessary. Add the ham, cover again
and leave to STAND while making the
omelette.

2   Whisk the egg whites in a large bowl
    until they are standing in soft peaks.
Beat the yolks with the skimmed milk,
pepper and marjoram or oregano.

3   Whisk 1 tablespoon of the egg whites
    into the yolk mixture, then quickly whisk
in the remainder.

4 Place the butter in a 25 cm/10 inch shallow flan dish. Cook on HIGH for 30 seconds. Pour in the omelette mixture.

5 Return to the microwave cooker and cook on MEDIUM for 3 minutes or until the mixture is partially set. Lift the edges with a spatula and spread out any uncooked egg evenly by tilting the dish. Cook on MEDIUM for 1 more minute or until the omelette sets.

6 Spoon the vegetable filling over the omelette. Fold the omelette in half and slide on to a hot serving plate. Dust with a little paprika.

7 Serve with wholemeal bread and a green salad.

To freeze: not suitable for freezing.

Notes: It is important to whisk the egg whites into the egg yolks quickly but thoroughly; take care, too, that the omelette does not overcook.

Variations
Use chopped mushrooms or onion slices instead of the vegetables.

| Fibre | ● | Sugar | |
| Fat | ● ● ● | Salt | ● |

Barbecue chicken nuggets

Serves 4
350 g/12 oz frozen chicken breast portions, defrosted
For the barbecue sauce
2 tablespoons tomato purée
1 teaspoon Worcestershire sauce
¼ teaspoon mustard powder
1 clove garlic, crushed
freshly ground black pepper
For the crunchy coating
25 g/1 oz wholemeal breadcrumbs
½ teaspoon each dried oregano, basil, thyme and paprika
1 teaspoon snipped fresh chives

1 Skin the chicken breasts, then cut them into pieces the size of a walnut. Mix the

barbecue sauce ingredients together then spoon the sauce over the chicken cubes until they are coated. Leave for 1 hour.

2 Meanwhile, mix the breadcrumbs with the herbs and spices then cook on HIGH for 5 minutes or until dry and crunchy, stirring once during the cooking time.

3 Arrange the chicken cubes in a shallow dish. Cook uncovered on HIGH for 4 minutes, rearranging the pieces of chicken halfway through the cooking time.

4 STAND for 2 minutes. Roll the hot chicken nuggets in the crunchy coating and serve immediately, with Sweetcorn and pepper relish (below).

To freeze: not suitable for freezing.

| Fibre | ● | Sugar | ● ● |
| Fat | ● | Salt | ● ● |

Sweetcorn and pepper relish

Serves 4
225 g/8 oz Mexican Mix, or an equivalent weight of fresh vegetables including diced red and green peppers, sweetcorn and chopped onion
2 tablespoons cider vinegar
50 ml/2 fl oz hot water
1 teaspoon cornflour
2 tablespoons water
1 teaspoon mustard
2 teaspoons honey

1 Place the Mexican Mix or fresh vegetables in a bowl with the cider vinegar and hot water. Cook, uncovered, on HIGH for 6 minutes.

2 Mix the cornflour with the water to form a smooth paste. Stir this into the relish with the mustard and honey, and cook on HIGH for 3 minutes. Cool fully.

To freeze: not suitable for freezing.

| Fibre | ● | Sugar | ● ● ● |
| Fat | | Salt | ● |

Spicy burgers

Makes 4
For the burgers
450 g/1 lb frozen minced beef,
defrosted
1 large onion, peeled and very finely
chopped
1 teaspoon black peppercorns, crushed
1 teaspoon coriander seeds, crushed
2 teaspoons chopped fresh marjoram
or 1 teaspoon dried oregano
1 tablespoon Worcestershire sauce
To serve
Wholemeal baps (page 42)
reduced fat mayonnaise (optional)
shredded lettuce
tomato and onion slices

1 Mix together all the burger ingredients until thoroughly blended.

2 Divide the mixture into 4 then shape into thick flat burgers about 9 cm/ 3½ inches in diameter.

3 Arrange the burgers on a large plate then cook uncovered on HIGH for 4 minutes.

4 Drain off the fat and juices, turn the burgers over, then cook for a further 2-3 minutes.

5 Spread the baps with mayonnaise, if liked, then fill with the burgers and salad before serving.

To freeze: wrap the burgers in cling film. Label and use within 2 months. To serve, place 2 at a time in the microwave cooker and reheat on HIGH for 5 minutes and serve as above.

Variation
To make cheese burgers, sprinkle a little grated cheese on top of each burger then brown under the grill.

Fibre	● ●	Sugar	●
Fat	● ●	Salt	● ●

Chili bean tacos

Serves 2-3

*100 g/4 oz frozen Mexican Mix, or an
   equivalent weight of fresh vegetables
   including diced red and green peppers,
   sweetcorn and chopped onion*
*432 g/15¼ oz can red kidney beans, juice
   reserved*
½ teaspoon Tabasco sauce
2 cloves garlic, crushed
2 tablespoons tomato purée
6 Mexican taco shells
1 small lettuce, cleaned and shredded
1 small fresh onion, peeled and chopped
50 g/ 2 oz Cheddar cheese, grated

1 Place the Mexican Mix or fresh
  vegetables in a serving dish. If using
fresh vegetables add 2 tablespoons water.
Cover with cling film, pierce, and cook on
HIGH for 3 minutes.

2 Stir the beans, Tabasco sauce, crushed
  garlic, and tomato purée into the
vegetables, then add enough of the reserved
juice to make a thick sauce. Cover again,
and cook for a further 3 minutes or until
tender.

3 Place the tacos on a serving plate then
  heat, uncovered, on HIGH for 1½
minutes or until hot.

4 Let people fill their own tacos. First
  spoon a few tablespoons of the bean
and vegetable mixture into the taco shells
then top with the lettuce, onion and cheese.
Eat with the fingers and have plenty of paper
napkins available.

To freeze: not suitable for freezing.

Fibre	● ● ●	**Sugar**	●	
Fat	●	**Salt**	● ● ●	

Left *Spicy burgers; Chili bean tacos*

Speedy spud snacks

Serves 2
2 potatoes, about 225 g/8 oz each, washed and dried

1 Prick the potatoes all over with a fork. Wrap them individually in a piece of absorbent kitchen paper and space them well apart in the microwave cooker.

2 Cook on HIGH for 6 minutes, turn the potatoes over and cook on HIGH for a further 5 minutes. STAND, wrapped in the absorbent kitchen paper for 5 minutes.

For the fillings
Cheese and chive filling: cut a thin slice from the top of each potato and scoop out the flesh into a bowl. Mash in 100 g/4 oz plain or flavoured cottage cheese, 2 tablespoons skimmed milk and 2 teaspoons chopped fresh chives. Season well and spoon the mixture back into the potato skins. Sprinkle with paprika and a few toasted almonds. Place on kitchen paper and cook on HIGH for 1 minute or until heated through.

To freeze: not suitable for freezing.

Fibre	○	Sugar	
Fat	○	Salt	○

BLT (bacon, lettuce and tomato) filling: derind 2 lean rashers of bacon and cut into strips. Place between 2 sheets of kitchen paper and cook on HIGH for 2 minutes or until crispy. Cool, then crumble the bacon. Cut a cross on the potatoes and pull the quarters apart. Spoon a handful of finely chopped Chinese leaves or crisp lettuce into each potato together with a tablespoon of reduced-calorie mayonnaise, 1 tomato, sliced, and 1 gherkin, sliced. Top with the crispy bacon and season well.

To freeze: not suitable for freezing.

Fibre	○	Sugar	○
Fat	○ ○	Salt	○ ○ ○

Nutty Hawaiian filling: mix 50 g/2 oz cooked chicken, diced, with 1 tomato,

skinned and chopped and 1 fresh peach, stoned and chopped or 2 pineapple rings, chopped. Stir in 4 tablespoons of low-calorie salad dressing or Piquant sauce (page 23) and season to taste with freshly ground black pepper. Split the potatoes across the top and spoon the filling into the splits.

To freeze: not suitable for freezing.

Fibre	○	Sugar	○
Fat	○ ○	Salt	○

Posh potato filling: soften 50 g/2 oz low fat soft cheese in the microwave cooker by cooking on MEDIUM for 30 seconds. Stir in 50 g/2 oz frozen smoked salmon, defrosted, and 50 g/2 oz frozen prawns, defrosted. Add 1-2 teaspoons capers or 4 stuffed green olives, sliced, and 1 tablespoon chopped fresh parsley. Season well. Split the potatoes across the top and spoon the filling into the splits. Sprinkle with paprika pepper and garnish with sprigs of parsley.

To freeze: not suitable for freezing.

Fibre	○	Sugar	
Fat	○ ○	Salt	○ ○ ○

Muffin pizzas

Serves 2
2 wholemeal muffins, halved
50 g/2 oz blue Brie or Stilton cheese
1 rasher lean bacon or ham, cut into strips
2 tomatoes, thickly sliced
freshly ground black pepper

1 Arrange the muffin halves on a plate. Spread or crumble the cheese on top, then add the bacon or ham strips followed by the tomato slices. Season well.

2 Cook on HIGH for 2 minutes. Transfer the muffin pizzas to a grill pan and place under a preheated hot grill for 1-2 minutes.

To freeze: not suitable for freezing.

Fibre	○ ○ ○	Sugar	○
Fat	○ ○	Salt	○ ○ ○

Sunshine eggs Florentine

Serves 2
*225 g/8 oz frozen chopped spinach,
  defrosted
25 g/1 oz mature Cheddar cheese, grated
2 eggs
freshly ground black pepper*

1 Divide the spinach between 2 shallow dishes. Cover with cling film, pierce, and cook on HIGH for 2 minutes. Remove the cling film.

2 Sprinkle the cheese on each dish then break an egg on top. Prick the egg yolk. Cover (see **Notes**) then cook on HIGH for 2 minutes. Season well and serve immediately.

To freeze: not suitable for freezing.

Notes: it is easier to use a special microwave plate cover or other suitable cover than cling film for this recipe. Using a small quantity of mature Cheddar cheese will give more flavour than using a larger quantity of low fat cheese.

Fibre	● ●	Sugar	●
Fat	● ●	Salt	●

Pitta pockets with tuna salad

Serves 4
2 wholemeal pitta breads
For the tuna salad
*198 g/7 oz can tuna in brine, drained
100 g/4 oz bean sprouts
6-8 black olives, stoned and chopped
5 cm/2 inch piece cucumber, chopped
50 g/2 oz frozen mixed sliced peppers
1 small onion, peeled and finely chopped
2 tomatoes, cut into wedges
1 tablespoon lemon juice
¼ teaspoon lemon rind (optional)
freshly ground black pepper*

1 Put the pitta bread between 2 pieces of absorbent kitchen paper then warm in the microwave cooker on HIGH for 30 seconds.

2 Place all the salad ingredients in a bowl. Cover with cling film, pierce, and cook on HIGH for 1½ minutes.

3 Cut the pitta bread in half across the centre and carefully open out to make 4 small pockets. Fill with the salad mixture and serve immediately.

To freeze: not suitable for freezing.

Fibre	● ● ●	Sugar	●
Fat	●	Salt	● ● ●

Lemon seafood avocado

Serves 4
*50 g/2 oz fresh wholemeal breadcrumbs
grated rind of 1 lemon
100 g/4 oz frozen peeled prawns, defrosted
5 tablespoons natural yogurt
freshly ground black pepper
2 large ripe avocados
1 tablespoon lemon juice
chopped fresh chives to garnish
curly endive, to serve*

1 Place the breadcrumbs in a bowl, and cook on HIGH for 5 minutes, or until crisp and dry.

2 Stir in the lemon rind, prawns, yogurt and black pepper. Mix well.

3 Cut the avocados in half. Remove and discard the stones, then sprinkle the flesh with lemon juice to stop it turning brown.

4 Pile the prawn mixture into each of the avocado halves. Arrange the avocado halves on a shallow dish, with their narrow ends pointing towards the centre. Cook on HIGH for 3½ minutes, rearranging the avocados halfway through the cooking time. Garnish each avocado half with chives. Serve immediately, on a bed of curly endive.

To freeze: not suitable for freezing.

Fibre	● ●	Sugar	●
Fat	● ● ●	Salt	●

HEALTHY MEALS FOR ONE OR TWO

It is always tempting, when cooking for one or two, to rely on quick snacks or take-aways. This chapter provides you with a range of wholesome recipes that you can make in advance, freeze in individual portions, and then thaw and reheat in the microwave cooker as and when you want.

Smoked mackerel kedgeree

Smoked mackerel kedgeree

Makes 2 individual servings
175 g/6 oz long grain American brown rice
grated rind and juice of 1 lemon
450 ml/¾ pint boiling water
*2× 75 g/3 oz frozen smoked mackerel fillets,
   defrosted*
2 teaspoons capers
4 tablespoons chopped fresh parsley
1 egg, hard-boiled and roughly chopped
To garnish
lemon wedges
sprigs of fresh parsley

1 Place the rice in a 1.75 litre/3 pint bowl with the lemon rind and juice. Pour over the boiling water. Cover with cling film, pierce, and cook on HIGH for 15 minutes. Stir once during the cooking time. Leave to STAND.

2 Cook the mackerel fillets on MEDIUM for 1 minute. Skin and flake the fish, then add it to the rice together with the remaining ingredients. Garnish with lemon wedges and sprigs of fresh parsley.

To freeze: spoon the kedgeree on to individual plates. Cover tightly with a double layer of cling film and label. Use within 1 month. To reheat from frozen, pierce the cling film then reheat one plate at a time on MEDIUM for about 5 minutes or until hot. Mix thoroughly with a fork then serve.

| Fibre | ● ● | Sugar | ● |
| Fat | ● ● | Salt | ● ● ● |

70

Corsican cannelloni

Corsican cannelloni

Makes 4 individual servings
about 750 ml/1 ¼ pints boiling water
½ teaspoon vegetable oil
8 sheets 'No-cook' lasagne verdi
225 g/8 oz frozen Ratatouille Mix or an
equivalent weight of fresh vegetables,
including tomatoes, aubergine,
courgettes, peppers and onions, diced
100 g/4 oz frozen broad beans
2 teaspoons chopped fresh mixed herbs
or 1 teaspoon dried mixed herbs
freshly ground black pepper
400 g/14 oz can chopped tomatoes
2 teaspoons Worcestershire sauce
100 g/4 oz mature Cheddar cheese, grated,
to serve

1 Pour the boiling water into a suitably shaped large shallow dish. Add a few drops of oil. Slide the sheets of lasagne into the dish and leave for 4-5 minutes to soften.

2 Put the ratatouille and beans in a medium-sized bowl. If using fresh vegetables, add 4 tablespoons water. Cover with cling film, pierce, and cook on HIGH for 4 minutes or until the vegetables soften. Drain well. Add the herbs and seasoning.

3 Lift out the lasagne sheets from the water and drain. Spread out on a clean working surface or large board. Divide the vegetable filling between the lasagne then neatly and carefully roll up the strips.

4 Divide half the can of tomatoes between 2 serving dishes. Placè 4 stuffed rolls close together on each dish. Spoon over the remaining tomatoes. Sprinkle with Worcestershire sauce. Cover with cling film.

5 To serve 2 individual servings immediately: pierce the cling film. Cook on HIGH for 5 minutes. Remove the cling film. Top with half the cheese and place the cannelloni under a preheated hot grill until brown.

To freeze: cover the cannelloni with a double layer of cling film and label. Freeze for up to 3 months. To reheat 2 individual servings from frozen, pierce the cling film. Cook on HIGH for 10 minutes. Remove the cling film then top with the 50 g/2 oz cheese. Place under a preheated hot grill to brown the cheese.

Fibre	• •	Sugar	•
Fat	• •	Salt	• • •

Potatossaka

Makes 6 individual servings
225 g/8 oz unpeeled potatoes, very thinly
*   sliced*
225 g/8 oz frozen sliced cabbage
1 tablespoon water
350 g/12 oz frozen minced beef
1 beef stock cube, crumbled
2 cloves garlic, crushed
100 g/4 oz frozen onion slices or 1 small
*   fresh onion, sliced*
¼-½ teaspoon ground allspice
½ teaspoon ground cinnamon
1 tablespoon tomato purée
freshly ground black pepper
For the cheese sauce
600 ml/1 pint skimmed milk
50 g/2 oz wholemeal flour
25 g/1 oz butter
75 g/3 oz Gouda or Edam cheese,
*   grated*

1 Put the potato and cabbage slices in a large bowl with the water. Cover with cling film, pierce, and cook on HIGH for 5 minutes.

2 Combine the frozen minced beef, crumbled stock cube, crushed garlic, onion slices, spices, tomato purée and pepper in a large bowl. Cover with cling film, pierce, and cook on HIGH for 6 minutes, stirring once during the cooking time.

3 To make the sauce, put the milk, flour, and butter in a large bowl and season with black pepper. Cook uncovered on HIGH for 2 minutes. Whisk well then cook for a further 6 minutes, stirring halfway through the cooking time. Stir in half the cheese.

4 Pour the spicy meat layer into the base of 6 individual pie dishes. Top each with the potato and cabbage then pour over the sauce, and smooth level.

5 Cover the dishes with cling film, pierce, and cook on HIGH for 8 minutes.

6 Remove the cling film then sprinkle over the remaining cheese. Brown under a preheated hot grill if liked.

To freeze: cover the dishes with a double layer of cling film then label. Use within 2 months. To reheat from frozen, pierce the cling film then reheat 1 portion at a time on HIGH for 10 minutes. If liked, brown under a preheated hot grill before serving.

Note: while the Potatossaka is reheating make a salad to serve with it. Use slices of tomato and onion, crisp lettuce or curly endive and a few stoned olives.

| Fibre | ○ | Sugar | ○ |
| Fat | ○ ○ | Salt | ○ ○ |

Chili con carne

Makes 4 individual servings
350 g/12 oz frozen minced beef
100 g/4 oz frozen onion slices or 1 small
*   fresh onion, sliced*
400 g/14 oz can peeled tomatoes, drained
*   and juice reserved*
2 cloves garlic, crushed
½ teaspoon ground cumin
1-2 teaspoons chili powder
1 beef stock cube
2 tablespoons wholemeal flour
425 g/15 oz can red kidney beans, drained

1 Place the meat, onion, tomatoes, garlic and spices in a bowl then crumble in the stock cube.

2 Stir well then cover with cling film and pierce. Cook on HIGH for 5 minutes stirring halfway through the cooking time.

3 Mix the flour with the reserved tomato juice and stir into the meat mixture. Cover again and cook for a further 3 minutes.

4 Stir in the beans then cook on HIGH for 5 minutes or until the mince is cooked. Allow the Chili con carne to cool, then skim off any fat that has risen to the surface.

To freeze: spoon the Chili con carne into individual bowls. Cover closely with a double layer of cling film and label. Use within 2 months. To reheat from frozen, pierce the cling film then thaw individual portions on

DEFROST for 8 minutes. Reheat on HIGH for 3 minutes. Two bowls of Chili con carne will take about 12 minutes to thaw on DEFROST, then reheat on HIGH for 5 minutes.

Fibre	● ●	Sugar	●
Fat	● ●	Salt	● ●

Plaice with watercress sauce

Serves 2
1 large fresh courgette
65 g/2½ oz packet fresh watercress,
*   washed, stalks removed*
15 g/½ oz butter
freshly ground black pepper
4 tablespoons natural yogurt
2 frozen plaice fillets
175 g/6 oz frozen Stewpack or an equivalent
*   weight of fresh vegetables, including*
*   onion, celery, swedes, turnips and*
*   carrots, peeled and diced*

1 Coarsely chop the courgette. Place in a large bowl with the watercress, butter and black pepper. Cover with cling film, pierce, and cook on HIGH for 4 minutes.

2 Cool for a few minutes, then transfer to a blender or food processor. Add the yogurt then process until almost smooth to make the watercress sauce.

3 Put the plaice fillets in the centre of 2 plates and surround with the vegetables. Cover with cling film and pierce. Cook on MEDIUM for 12-13 minutes.

4 Pour the sauce into a small bowl, cover with cling film, pierce, and cook on HIGH for 2 minutes. Spoon over the fish and vegetables.

To freeze: do not freeze the fish or vegetables, but make and freeze the sauce in advance. Pour the sauce into 1 or 2 plastic containers, leaving 2.5 cm/1 inch headspace. Label. Use within 1 month. To reheat from frozen, thaw the sauce on DEFROST for 5 minutes. Turn out of the container into a bowl. Leave to STAND while

cooking the fish and vegetables according to step 3. Cover the sauce with cling film, pierce, and cook on HIGH for 2 minutes, then spoon over the fish and vegetables.

Note: plastic plate rings are useful for separating plates in the microwave cooker: 2 dishes can be stacked and cooked at once.

Fibre	●	Sugar	●
Fat	● ●	Salt	●

Seville turkey

Makes 4 individual servings
750 g/1½ lb frozen boneless diced turkey,
*   defrosted*
freshly ground black pepper
grated rind of 1 orange
25 g/1 oz butter
50 ml/2 fl oz orange juice
50 ml/2 fl oz sherry
1 orange, peeled and sliced, to garnish

1 Place the diced turkey in a shallow casserole dish and sprinkle with the pepper. Cover with cling film, pierce, and cook on HIGH for 6 minutes, stirring twice during the cooking period. Set aside.

2 Place the orange rind, butter, orange juice and sherry in a jug. Cook on HIGH, uncovered, for 3 minutes, stirring once during cooking.

3 Drain any juice from the diced turkey, then pour over the hot orange and sherry sauce. If serving immediately, cook, uncovered, on HIGH for 2 more minutes, then serve, garnished with the orange slices.

To freeze: allow to cool fully after mixing the orange and sherry sauce and the diced turkey together, then pack in 4 individual serving dishes. Cover, label and freeze: use within 3 months. To thaw, place 2 serving dishes in the microwave cooker and cook on HIGH for 10 minutes. Garnish with orange slices before serving.

Fibre	●	Sugar	● ●
Fat	● ● ●	Salt	●

Simple wholemeal pizza

Serves 2
For the pizza base
225 g/8 oz wholemeal self-raising flour
1 teaspoon baking powder
1 teaspoon dried mixed herbs
freshly ground black pepper
40 g/1 ½ oz butter
1 egg beaten
85 ml/3 fl oz skimmed milk

For the topping
1 small onion, peeled and very thinly sliced
100 g/4 oz frozen sliced mushrooms,
* defrosted and drained*
2 tomatoes, sliced
25 g/1 oz lean ham, chopped
1 tablespoon chopped walnuts
100 g/4 oz Gouda cheese, grated

1 Mix the flour, baking powder, half the herbs and black pepper together, then rub in the butter until the mixture resembles fine breadcrumbs.

2 Add the beaten egg and milk and mix to a soft dough. Cut the dough in half.

3 Lightly flour a work surface and roll out the dough with a rolling pin to make two 20 cm/8 inch rounds.

4 Line two plates or suitable microwave dishes with greaseproof paper. Carefully lift the pizza bases on to the plates. Cook 1 pizza base at a time, uncovered, on HIGH for 1 ½-2 minutes or until risen and just dry on the surface.

5 Carefully lift the pizza bases and paper off the plates and wipe away the moisture on the plates. Return to the plates.

6 Scatter the onion and mushrooms over each base then sprinkle over the remaining herbs. Cook each one uncovered on HIGH for 2 minutes. Arrange the remaining ingredients on top and cook on HIGH for a further 3 minutes.

To freeze: cool then overwrap each plate with cling film and label. Use within 2 months. To reheat from frozen, remove the cling film then reheat, 1 pizza at a time on HIGH for 4 minutes or until thawed and heated through.

| Fibre | ● ● ● | Sugar | ● |
| Fat | ● ● | Salt | ● ● ● |

Oriental chicken

Makes 4 individual servings
450 g/1 lb frozen Oriental Mix or an equivalent
* weight of fresh vegetables, including*
* beansprouts, water chestnuts, sweetcorn,*
* sliced mushrooms, sliced red peppers,* •
* sliced beans and bamboo shoots*
350 g/12 oz cooked chicken, cut into strips
8 tablespoons Chinese plum stir-fry sauce.

Simple wholemeal pizza

Oriental chicken

1. Mix the frozen or fresh vegetables and chicken in a large bowl. Add the plum sauce then stir until evenly coated.

2. Spoon into 4 individual serving dishes or on to plates, then cover closely with cling film. To serve, pierce the cling film then reheat, one portion at a time on HIGH for 5 minutes or until hot and the vegetables are cooked, but are still crisp.

To freeze: label and place in freezer. Use within 1 month. To serve, proceed as above.

Note: Chinese-style plum sauce can be made very easily. Place 225 g/8 oz stoned, chopped fresh plums in a bowl with a small, deseeded and finely chopped green chili,

50 g/2 oz finely chopped dried apricots and a teaspoon of chopped stem ginger. Stir in 3 tablespoons of white wine vinegar, 1 crushed clove of garlic and a tablespoon of brown sugar. Cover with cling film, pierce, and cook on HIGH for 10 minutes or until the mixture has softened. Stir once during cooking. Cool, pour into a sterilized screw-top jar and store in the refrigerator for up to 3 weeks.

Variations
This recipe can be made using slivers of cooked pork, duck or beef, but the fat content is higher than when using chicken.

Fibre	●	Sugar	● ●
Fat	●	Salt	● ●

Macaroni supper

Makes 4 individual servings
175 g/6 oz wholemeal macaroni
900 ml/1 ½ pints boiling water
3 rashers frozen lean bacon, defrosted,
rinded and chopped
175 g/6 oz frozen sliced courgettes
50 g/2 oz frozen mixed sliced peppers
2 tomatoes, skinned and roughly chopped
For the sauce
300 ml/½ pint skimmed milk
25 g/1 oz wholemeal flour
½ teaspoon mustard powder
freshly ground black pepper
25 g/1 oz butter
For the topping
100 g/4 oz Edam or Cheddar cheese, grated
½ teaspoon chili powder

1 Put the macaroni into a 2.75 litre/5 pint bowl. Pour in the boiling water, cover with a plate and cook on HIGH for 5 minutes. Keep covered and leave to STAND.

2 Put the chopped bacon, courgettes, peppers and tomato into a medium-sized bowl. Cover with cling film, pierce, and cook on HIGH for 4 minutes. Set aside.

3 To make the sauce, whisk the milk, flour, mustard powder and seasoning in a bowl. Add the butter. Cook on HIGH for 4 minutes, stirring halfway through the cooking time.

4 Drain the macaroni and stir in the sauce. Spoon half the macaroni into 4 individual bowls. Spoon the vegetable mixture on the top, then spoon on the remaining macaroni. Sprinkle the cheese and chili powder over the top and brown under a preheated hot grill. Serve immediately.

To freeze: cool then cover with a double layer of cling film and label. Use within 2 months. To reheat from frozen, pierce the cling film. Reheat 1 dish on HIGH for 5 minutes or 2 dishes on HIGH for 9 minutes. When heated through, remove the cling film and brown under a preheated hot grill, if liked.

Note: for extra speed, boil the macaroni conventionally while cooking the vegetables and sauce in the microwave cooker.

Variation
For a vegetarian meal, add 3 tablespoons red kidney beans instead of the bacon.

| Fibre | ● ● ● | Sugar | ● |
| Fat | ● ● | Salt | ● ● ● |

Mexican peppers

Makes 4 individual servings
4 medium size peppers, tops sliced off and
deseeded
4 tablespoons water
For the filling
100 g/4 oz frozen onion slices or 1 small
fresh onion, peeled and sliced
2-3 dried chili peppers, snipped with
scissors
100 g/4 oz long grain brown rice
15 g/½ oz butter
450 m/¾ pint hot vegetable stock
100 g/4 oz frozen sweetcorn
100 g/4 oz frozen peas
100 g/4 oz lean cooked ham, cut into strips
4 tablespoons chili relish

1 Arrange the peppers and tops in a deep dish with the water. Cover loosely with cling film, pierce, and cook on HIGH for 4 minutes. Drain and set aside.

2 Place the onion, dried chilies, rice and butter in a 2.75 litre/5 pint bowl. Cover with cling film, pierce, and cook on HIGH for 2 minutes. Stir in 300 ml/½ pint of the hot stock. Cover again and cook on HIGH for a further 8 minutes.

3 Stir in the vegetables and ham and more stock if necessary. Cover again and cook on HIGH for a further 5-6 minutes or until the rice is almost cooked but is still moist.

4 Stir in the relish. Fill each pepper with the rice mixture. Cover with cling film, pierce, and cook on HIGH for 5 minutes. Rearrange the peppers, replace their tops,

cover again and cook on HIGH for a further 5 minutes.

To freeze: cool the peppers then wrap individually in cling film and label. Use within 2 months. To reheat from frozen, unwrap and put on individual plates. Reheat 1 pepper on HIGH for 4½ minutes or 2 peppers on HIGH for 8 minutes.

Variation
For a vegetarian filling, substitute chopped toasted cashew nuts instead of the ham, and add to the cooked vegetables and rice with the chili relish.

Fibre	● ● ●	Sugar	●
Fat	● ●	Salt	● ● ●

Chunky lentil soup

Makes 4 individual servings
100 g/4 oz dried red lentils
225 g/8 oz frozen onion slices or 2 small fresh onions, sliced
1 teaspoon ground coriander
1 teaspoon ground cumin
2-3 cloves garlic, crushed
3 tablespoons tomato purée
600 ml/1 pint boiling vegetable or chicken stock
freshly ground black pepper
225 g/8 oz frozen Stewpack vegetables or an equivalent weight of fresh root vegetables, including carrots, swedes, turnips, onions and celery, trimmed and diced

1 Place the lentils in a large bowl with the onion, coriander, cumin, crushed garlic and tomato purée.

2 Pour in the boiling stock and mix well. Add plenty of black pepper then cover with cling film, pierce, and cook on HIGH for 10 minutes.

3 Stir the vegetables into the lentil mixture, cover again then cook for a further 10 minutes or until the vegetables and lentils are tender. Serve immediately with wholemeal bread rolls.

To freeze: cool, then spoon the soup into serving bowls or microwave dishes. Cover tightly with cling film and label. Use within 2 months. To reheat from frozen, pierce the cling film then reheat one bowl at a time on HIGH for about 8 minutes, stirring as the soup begins to thaw. To reheat two bowls from frozen, pierce the cling film then reheat on HIGH for about 15-17 minutes, stirring as the soup begins to thaw.

Fibre	● ● ●	Sugar	●
Fat	●	Salt	●

Mushrooms with garlic and yogurt sauce

Makes 4 individual servings
450 g/1 lb frozen whole small or button mushrooms, defrosted
2 teaspoons chopped fresh parsley
2 large cloves garlic, crushed
1 tablespoon lemon juice
1 teaspoon cornflour
5 tablespoons natural yogurt
15 g/½ oz butter
freshly ground black pepper

1 Place the mushrooms in a large bowl. Cover, pierce, and cook on HIGH for 4 minutes, stirring halfway through the cooking time. Drain off all excess liquid.

2 Mix in the parsley, garlic and lemon juice. Cover again, pierce, and cook on HIGH for a further 2 minutes.

3 Mix the cornflour into the yogurt. Add the yogurt mixture, butter and pepper to the mushrooms and cook, uncovered, on HIGH for 2 more minutes, stirring once. Serve immediately with slices of fresh wholemeal bread.

To freeze: allow to cool fully, then pack in 4 individual serving dishes. Cover, label and freeze: use within 1 month. To thaw, place 1 serving dish in the microwave cooker and cook on HIGH for 4-5 minutes, or until hot.

Fibre	● ●	Sugar	●
Fat	●	Salt	●

MENU MAKER

This section is designed to show some of the possibilities that exist for composing attractive, wholesome and healthy menus from the many recipes that are included in this book. Planning a whole menu can seem a daunting task, so you'll be pleased to see how easily different strands of the book work together to produce a healthy meal for all sorts of occasions.

Here are some examples of the varied menus that you can create: use the index on page 80 to locate the recipes.

SPRING LUNCH FOR FOUR

Sole and smoked salmon rolls

Farmhouse turkey in wine and mustard
Spring leaf parcels

Brightly glazed apples

SUMMER DINNER FOR FOUR

Mushrooms and onions à la grecque

Lamb, coriander and courgette kebabs
Perfect brown rice

Rhubarb summer puddings

AUTUMN LUNCH FOR SIX

Chicken pâté ring

Glazed lamb with apricots
Aubergine and potato timbale

Red fruit and ginger fool

WINTER DINNER FOR FOUR

Mulligatawny soup

Pork rolls with apple and prune stuffing
Barley bake

Cherry cheesecake

SUMMER PICNIC FOR SIX

St. Clement's carrot soup

Creamed smoked haddock pâté

Sesame chicken
Fish, tomato and walnut salad
A selection of salads

Tropical fruitcake

Left *Sesame chicken (page 57);* **Right** *Spicy burgers (page 66);* **Above right** *Raspberry and orange sorbet (page 52)*

HALLOWE'EN SUPPER FOR FOUR

Pitta pockets with tuna salad

Autumn marrow
Speedy spud snacks
Herby corn cobs

ST. VALENTINE'S DAY DINNER FOR TWO

Rainbow trout with watercress and almonds

Oriental chicken
Sweet and sour vegetables with cashews

Raspberry and orange sorbet

BIRTHDAY TEA FOR EIGHT

Wholemeal baps
Cheesy topped wholemeal scones

Frosted coconut and carrot loaf
Nutty shortbread
Ginger fingers
Honey and banana cake

Gooseberry and strawberry meringue

INSTANT DINNER FOR FOUR

Sunshine eggs Florentine

Devilled chicken livers
Speedy spud snacks

LATE NIGHT SUPPER FOR FOUR

Tandoori-style chicken
Spinach, cauliflower and courgette bhaji

Tropical fruit salad

SATURDAY LUNCH FOR FOUR

Fish, tomato and walnut salad

Spicy burgers
Green salad

Fruit medley

SUNDAY LUNCH FOR FOUR

Creamed smoked haddock pâté

Rosemary lamb
Layered potato and apple bake
Courgette twists

Fruity sponge pudding with marmalade sauce

INDEX